TO STEPHANIE,

BEST ALWAYS,

Finding It Again

February Press, LLC

FINDING IT AGAIN

The Truth About Love After 40

by

Kenn Shapiro

ISBN 978-0-9801151-0-9

First Edition 2008

Published by
February Press, LLC

For Jason and Laura,
of course

TABLE OF CONTENTS

PREFACE

He was laughing, so I didn't take him seriously.

He was Steve Cassel, Ph.D. At the time, he had been my shrink for about six years. I'd started seeing him in the early part of 1997, as my marriage was in its final days, and I continued to see him, weekly, through the ensuing years of tumult and turmoil and pain. With a willing ear and a steady demeanor, he'd listened and counseled during what seemed like a rapid-fire stream of one emotional crisis after another. By the early part of 2000, my therapy had been influenced and impacted by the separation from my wife of 17 years, our subsequent divorce, her sudden diagnosis with a terminal illness, her passing, and the effects of all of this on my two teenaged children.

Any of these crises could form the basis for a book. The pain of separation, the ugliness of divorce, the horror of an ex-spouse's terminal illness (particularly when the recent acrimony leaves no room for any rapprochement), the grief and the sorrow of teenaged children coming to terms, over such a short period of time, with divorce and then the death of a parent—I could write hundreds of pages on each of these topics, and maybe someday I will.

But not today.

Today I want to write about love. More specifically, love after forty. And about Steve Cassel's laughter.

A few months after my separation, I started dating. My efforts at first were hesitant (the natural consequence of inexperience), with many periods of interruption (attributable, understandably, to the cascading crises confronting me). But just as he was there to help me find my way through the dark emotional traumas, so was Steve Cassel there to hear me vent about the world of middle-aged dating.

Initially, our sessions were overwhelmingly serious, focused as they should have been on the sober concerns occasioned by divorce and illness and death, with only the occasional lighthearted mention of a dating issue. Gradually, though, as time and crises passed, and as the emotional urgency lessened, the scales began to shift, and I found myself spending more and more time in each session recounting my most recent dating experiences. Like any good psychologist, Steve would listen more than he would talk, gleaning insight and data not so much from the topic of my monologues, but from the detail and the nuance of what I was saying. Still, despite his highly professional manner and his studied concentration during our sessions, every once in a while (and with a growing frequency as my dating stories increased), he'd be unable to resist the impulse to laugh.

"I'm sorry," he would say, the first few times it happened, "I'm not laughing at you, I'm just laughing at the story." I believed him, of course. My therapy had revealed a host of neuroses, but low self-esteem and paranoia were not among them. After a time, though, the apologies became unnecessary, as Steve grew increasingly comfortable indulging his laugh reflex while I journalistically reported one ridiculous dating escapade after another.

Then came that fateful day, some six years into our patient-therapist relationship, when he followed up his laughter with a suggestion.

"You know," he said, still catching his breath after the details of a particularly outlandish episode, "you really should be writing these stories down."

* * *

I ignored his suggestion at first. Every unmarried, forty-something adult in America has an inventory of laugh-inducing, shrink-choking tales about dating, but that doesn't mean we should all be putting them on paper. Without a broader story to tell, a compendium of dating yarns is the literary equivalent of a six-pack of Diet Coke—refreshing, perhaps, but of no nutritional value—and no one wants to ingest 200 pages of Diet Coke. My dating stories may have been entertaining, but at the time of Steve's suggestion, they were nothing more than a collection of amusing but otherwise pointless anecdotes.

That has changed. Though my weekly sessions with Steve eventually came to an end, my efforts at finding romance continued. And in the ongoing, repetitive, years-long process of living through date after date, episode after episode, relationship after relationship, a curious and unexpected phenomenon emerged: Eventually, I began to distill some important truths about that elusive little gem we all call love. This, in turn, made me realize that through the cumulative effect of my experiences, I actually did, indeed, have a broader tale to tell, and that Steve was right: I really should be writing these stories down.

And so I have.

* * *

Steve Cassel is a real person—an eminent psychologist who helped me discover more facets of myself than I ever knew existed—and the story of his inspiring laughter is one hundred percent true. This book is constructed around other stories—the stories of various dates and relationships I've experienced in my recent years as a man older than 40. For the most part, these other stories are also true. I say, "For the most part," for two reasons: First because, as a writer, I've been trained to embellish for effect (don't believe any writer who claims not to embellish), so I have, in fact,

3

taken liberties with the truth when the flow of a story required it. Mainly, though, I use the qualifier, "For the most part," because, as a lawyer, I want to avoid being sued.

This second reason also explains why, in all of the stories about dating and relationships, the names, places, landmarks, and other aspects that might serve to identify any person other than myself have been changed. If someone I've previously dated reads this book, thinks she recognizes herself, and is pleased and flattered with the way she's been portrayed, then yes, it's entirely possible that that particular story is about her. If, on the other hand, she thinks she recognizes herself in a story and is furious about the way she's been depicted, then she should rest assured that no, the story was not about her—it was obviously an embellished, exaggerated account about someone else.

* * *

As I revealed in the story about Steve, my first few years in therapy coincided with events far larger and more demanding than my search for love and romance. Except for a passing reference here and there when required in the context of a story, this book is not about those events. But don't be fooled. Although this book has a singular focus, my dating adventures were but a part of a much fuller schedule of serious obligations, responsibilities, and challenges. Throughout it all, nothing has been more important to me than my role as parent of the two kindest, warmest, most loving, most responsible human beings I know. Nothing within my life has ever occupied a higher priority.

This book, therefore, is not so much an all-inclusive memoir as it is a focused journal, a chronicle highlighting one aspect of a very complicated but enlightening time in my life. Some of the stories may be funny. Others, maybe not so much. In the end, though, this book is more than a mere collection of stories. The stories are chapters in what I hope is a broader tale, a tale about one man's trek toward a version of wisdom and truth. In many ways, it's a tale about a journey and a quest. Where am I going on the journey? What am I seeking in the quest? Do I get there? Do I find it?

Read on.

PART ONE

INITIATION

CHAPTER ONE—YOU NEVER KNOW

I had been separated for about four months when my friend, Helen Eisenberg, called to ask whether I was ready to start dating.

Hmm, I thought . . . dating?

In the abstract, of course, I knew what that meant. Going out with women. Dinner, dancing, shows, movies, romance, sex, maybe even love. Everyone knows what "dating" means, right? The fact, though, is that although I was, at the time, a 40-year-old man, I had never actually "dated" as an adult. I'd had a girlfriend or two in high school, then a "serious" relationship throughout most of college and law school, and then, at 22, I met the woman who would eventually become my wife. I had no "single" period as an adult, no time when I was out there, on my own, without a mate, going to bars, getting fixed up, meeting women at the local supermarket or on singles cruises or wherever else single adults found each other. From the time in my teens when I first started shaving, I had pretty much been involved in one relationship or another, and now here I was, at 40, recently separated after 17 years of marriage, being asked by a friend if I was ready to start doing something I'd never done before, but which, by her tone of voice, she made to seem as basic and simple as walking or breathing.

There was no big build-up in Helen's question, no hesitation in her voice, no indication from her that her call involved something dangerous or thrilling or new. It was very matter-of-fact, as though she were calling someone who'd just gotten over a 24-hour stomach bug: "Hi, Kenn, it's Helen. How's your stomach? Better? Good. Ready to start eating yet?" Except it was, "Hi, Kenn, how you doing? Listen, it's been four months—are you ready to start dating yet?"

In retrospect, I realize Helen was as clueless as I was. About 10 years older than I, Helen had been married to my friend, Larry, for more than 25 years, so her frame of reference on the realities of middle-aged dating was even less informed than mine, but the nonchalant, almost cavalier, tone of her voice—"Ready to start dating yet?"—disarmed me. Dating. How hard could it be? Hmmm. Before I'd finished all the mental gymnastics involved in deciding whether I was, in fact, really ready, I heard myself answering Helen: "Sure. Why not?"

"Great," Helen said, and then she launched right in, fast: "My friend, Robin, has a friend. She's a legal secretary, 38 years old, petite, blonde—really, really cute—divorced, with one son maybe 7 or 8 years old. Her name is Naomi, she lives one town over from you, and she's waiting for your call. Here's her number. Call her now."

* * *

I live in Coral Springs, Florida. It's a suburb of Fort Lauderdale, in the northwest corner of Broward County. There's neither any coral nor any springs in Coral Springs, Florida. For that matter, there's no fort in Fort Lauderdale. There's not a single hill in the entire city of Lauderhill, nor are there any natural lakes in the town of Lauderdale Lakes. None of that matters—in South Florida, everything has a pretty name.

* * *

I wrote down Naomi's phone number, thanked Helen, then sat down at the kitchen table with the phone in one hand, Naomi's number in the other, and a sense of nervous panic slowly draining the blood from my toes and my fingers.

"What the hell do I do now?" I thought. Just moments earlier, prior to Helen's call, I had been wrestling with the vexing issue of whether to heat up some of Mrs. Paul's frozen fish sticks for dinner, or splurge and call in for some Chinese food. Now, notwithstanding the cool 72 degree breeze blowing in from the terrace, my armpits were sweating, my appetite was gone, my throat was dry, and I was staring at the phone number of a really, really cute legal secretary who was, at that very minute, waiting for my call.

Gulp.

I looked at my watch. It was about twenty after 6. Well, I thought, it's suppertime. I certainly can't call Naomi now—she's probably in the middle of dinner, and it would be unfair and awkward to make that first call while she's eating. I'll wait a little while, like until 7:30. Yeah, 7:30. That'd be a good time to call.

For the next hour I found myself regularly checking my watch, at intervals that seemed like eons but which actually averaged about every 5 minutes, until, finally, as 7:20 rolled around, I walked over to the phone, stared at it, and wondered to myself, "Okay, what are you gonna say to this woman when you call her ten minutes from now?"

I hadn't come up with anything as 7:30 approached, so I convinced myself that 7:30 was actually a terrible time to call. Helen said Naomi had a young child—7 or 8 years old—and I remembered, from when my own kids were that age, that 7:30, for a 7 or 8-year-old, was prime getting-ready-for-bed time, so calling Naomi at 7:30 would surely be interrupting some pre-bedtime routine. No, 7:30 would be a terrible time to call. I should probably wait until 8:30—by then, her son would be comfortably tucked in, and we could chat the night away without any interference. Yeah, that's it: 8:30. That's when I'll call.

From 7:30 until 8:30, I sat on my sofa with the phone in my lap, watching the clock on my wall as the minutes ticked away in slow motion, wondering what I would say to this woman when I finally picked up the nerve to make the call. I was 40 years old—a grown man, a professional, a father, a veteran of 17 years of marriage—and I had never before been in this position: Calling up a grown woman I'd never met, and asking her out for a date. What was I going to say? How was I going to start? Should I just introduce myself and say, "Would you like to have dinner one night?" No—too abrupt! How about, "Hi, Naomi, this is Kenn Shapiro, Helen gave me your number and said you might like to have dinner sometime. Would you?" That might work—it gets to the point soon enough, so I don't end up hemming and hawing like some rookie, and adding the stuff about getting the number from Helen makes it a little less direct, right? Nah—still too lame! Where's the personality? I've got to show this woman I have a personality. Yeah, that's it—use my personality!

Okay—but how?

8:30 rolled around, and still I had nothing—how does one put one's personality into a script?—so I convinced myself that 8:30 was a bad time to call. Calling exactly on the hour or the half-hour, I decided, would give me away as nervous and inexperienced—it would suggest that I had decided ahead of time exactly when I would call, and that I'd been pacing around, waiting for the clock to hit that exact moment, like some idiotic dolt who had never asked a woman out on a date before, which was, of course, painfully true, but too pathetic for me to let on by calling at a time that would give that all away. No—calling on the half-hour would send the wrong message. I should call at a time that would seem as though I just randomly, casually, non-nervously picked up the phone, without forethought. It should seem as though I just happened to be walking by the phone during my busy evening routine and, seeing the phone, decided, without much contemplation, "Oh, you know what, let me call that woman Helen told me about and see if she'd like to grab a bite one night." Yes, yes, yes—that's it! That's how it should come across.

So what time should I call to make it seem as though that's exactly what happened?

I thought for a minute or two, and then I decided. 8:48. That's when I would call. 8:48. It wasn't on the hour or the half-hour. It wasn't at a convenient five-minute interval. It was a random time, in between the markers on any clock or watch, and would send the unmistakable message to Naomi that I had not been sitting around like a twit trying to pick up the nerve to make this call, but that instead, with confidence and a casual air, I had picked up the phone the first chance I had after going through my evening routine.

Great. Okay. 8:48. That was it. No ifs, ands, or buts, that was definitely the time I was going to make the call. Still, while successfully stealing another 18 minutes of delay, I had yet to solve the dilemma of how, actually, to break the ice. What would I say? "Hello, is this Naomi?" Of course it is, you moron—who else would it be? But what if her son picked up the phone? Do I say, "Is Naomi home?" Too formal to say to a 7 or 8-year-old. How about, "Is your mommy home?" Too familiar. What about, "Is your mom home?" Yeah—good. That's good. Is your mom home. Okay. But then what if the kid says, "Who is this?" Okay— I'll say, "This is Kenn Shapiro." But then what if he says, "Can I tell her what you're calling about?" Well, I'll say that I got her number from Helen, who knows Robin, who

13

thought we might like to meet each other and maybe get together and . . . oh, for crying out loud, no 7 or 8-year-old will ask what I'm calling about!

I looked at the clock. It was 8:47. Oh my god. For all the rehearsing and preparing and worrying and pacing, I still had no idea how to get this conversation started, and I had less than a minute to figure it all out. Then I glanced at the clock once again, and there it was, staring at me, undeniably: 8:48.

The moment of truth had arrived. A thousand voices screamed inside my head: "Wait." "Don't call yet." "Think up another reason for delay." "You're not ready." "You don't know what to say."

And then, somehow, from somewhere, it came over me—a feeling of resolve. Perhaps my psyche had just surrendered to the exhaustion of all the mental calisthenics of the past couple of hours, but suddenly I found myself thinking, "Oh, screw it, already—just do it." And with that, I took a deep breath, picked up the phone, dialed the number, and, having absolutely no idea what I was really going to say, I listened as a sweet-sounding woman's voice on the other end said, simply, "Hello?"

And then, like a car on cruise control, some portion of my brain—some unfamiliar area within the deep folds and recesses—took over.

"Is this Naomi?" I asked.

"Yes."

"Hi, Naomi, this is Kenn Shapiro. I got your number from my friend, Helen, who knows your friend, Robin. Look, Naomi, the last time I called to ask someone out on a date, Jimmy Carter was President. And the last time I called to ask someone out on a *blind* date was, um, never. So if I seem a little unpracticed at this, it's only because I am."

Looking back on it now I still don't know where it came from—certainly, it was not the stilted introduction I had rehearsed. Apparently, though, I do have a personality, and when I allowed myself to get out of my own way for that brief half-a-minute or so, it found its way to the surface. Naomi laughed at my Jimmy Carter reference, we commiserated for a minute or two on the difficulties of dating after marriage, and, the ice having been broken and now melting away rapidly, we talked about anything and everything for more than an hour.

We talked about our kids, we talked about our work, we talked about where we grew up and where we went to school. We talked about where we lived now, about our hobbies, about the places we'd been and the things we'd seen. We talked and talked until, at a certain point, it seemed appropriate for me to suggest that we continue our conversation in person, perhaps, say, over dinner sometime.

"Sure," said Naomi, "that'd be great."

So we picked a place to meet, and settled on a date and time. Then, not wanting Naomi to know that Helen had already described her to me—I thought it would seem shallow that I called only after such a flattering physical description, and even though it was true, I didn't think it was proper for Naomi to know so soon how shallow I really was—I asked, "So tell me, when I get to the restaurant, how will I recognize you?"

"Well," she said, with me only halfway listening, since I'd already been told what she looked like, "I'm about five foot three, petite, brown hair, and I'll be wearing a blue top."

"Okay," I said. I described myself, told her what I'd be wearing, told her how much I was looking forward to our date, then said good night, hung up the phone, and like an athlete who had just won a championship, I thrust my arms in the air, gleeful and victorious.

* * *

"That was great!" I thought to myself. "You did it! You made the call! You were charming! You were witty! You didn't stammer or stutter—you had a free and easy conversation with a cute, 38-year-old legal secretary who has agreed to go out on a date with you! You broke that 'never done this before' barrier—broke it with a battering ram—and you came through without a nick, without a scratch, without a scar! This is amazing!"

And then it hit me.

Brown hair?

Did she just say she had brown hair? I mean, I don't really have a preference for one hair color over any other, but I'm pretty sure Helen said this woman had blonde hair. Why would Naomi now say she had brown hair? Let me just call Helen to make sure I heard correctly.

Helen was glad to hear from me. "So," she said, "did you call? How'd it go?"

"Yes," I said, "I called, and it went really well. We talked for over an hour. I can't believe I actually made the call, but once we got started talking it just took off from there. We're having dinner a few nights from now."

"Wow," said Helen, "I'm so excited!"

"Me, too," I said, "and thank you. I have one question for you, though."

"What's the question?"

"Remember you said that she had blonde hair?"

"Yeah," said Helen "blonde, petite, really really cute."

"Well," I said, "this woman says she has brown hair."

Helen was silent for two or three seconds, then, sounding puzzled, said, "Brown hair?"

"Yes," I said, "she said she was five-three, petite, with brown hair. She definitely said 'brown hair.'"

Helen was perplexed. "Let me call Robin, I'll find out what's going on," she said. "I'll call you right back."

Four minutes later, the phone rang. It was Helen.

"Kenny," she said, and then, after a less-than-comforting pause, "um, I don't quite know how to tell you this."

"Tell me what?" I asked.

"Well," she said, somewhat gingerly, as if expecting a bad reaction, "it looks like I gave you the wrong number."

Now the pause was mine.

"Excuse me?" I said, not quite believing what I was hearing.

"Well," Helen continued, "as it turns out, Robin has two divorced legal secretary friends. I didn't know that. I've only met the blonde one. So when I asked Robin for the phone number of her divorced legal secretary friend, I was asking for the number of the cute blonde, but she just assumed I was asking for the other one, so she gave me the phone number for the brunette."

"So who did I just make a date with?" I asked.

"Well, here's the thing," Helen started. Whenever someone starts a sentence with "here's the thing," you just know the "thing" you're about to hear is not a good one. Helen continued: "Robin says she's not pretty . . . but she's attractive."

Huh?

"What does that mean?" I asked, not quite panicked, but obviously a tad concerned.

"Well," Helen said, "I never met this woman, so I don't know firsthand, but you know how someone can be attractive without necessarily being pretty, right? You see people all the time, don't you, who are maybe not quite beauty queens but are still very attractive, right?"

"Uh, yeah, I guess," I said, with some hesitation, mainly because I was lying—the truth is that I was having a hard time accepting that any woman could qualify as "attractive" while simultaneously being "not pretty."

"So don't worry," she said, "I'm sure you'll have a wonderful time."

I hung up the phone. Worried.

I had just made a date with a woman based on the recommendation of a trusted friend who, it turns out, had never actually met, spoken with, nor even heard of the person she had just set me up with. While it was true that I didn't make the date until I'd spoken with Naomi for over an hour—and while she certainly sounded nice enough over the phone—it is also true that I doubt I ever would have made the call if Helen had told me up front that Naomi was "not pretty, but attractive." As superficial as it may sound, virtually every crucial aspect of the evening had been influenced by the fact that I thought I was calling someone who was "really, really cute." My nervousness, my trepidation, my preparation, my exhilaration—all were partly prompted, and certainly enhanced, by my belief that Naomi was a looker. Now, I wasn't so sure. Was the conversation really as great as I initially thought it was? The topics, after all, were somewhat generic, and we barely brushed the surface, hopping around as we did from subject to subject. Was she truly interesting, or could I even know such a thing after a conversation so relatively brief and light? Was I really excited about the prospect of meeting Naomi? Or did my excitement spring from the more abstract notion of getting to meet a "really, really cute" woman—any "really, really cute" woman?

Not pretty. But attractive. What did that mean?

Our date was three nights away, so I spent the next three days trying to see if I could pick out women who were "not pretty," but "attractive." At the grocery store, at the video store, at work, in parking lots—every where I went, I tried to isolate at least one female face that I could fairly describe as being not quite pretty, but certainly attractive.

I was having a very difficult time.

The difference, at least for me, required an appreciation for subtlety of which I was apparently incapable. To me, Neanderthal as it may sound, "pretty" equaled "attractive," and "not pretty" equaled "not attractive." Anything else—any effort to switch the variables in either of those equations—simply defied the laws of mathematics, and my efforts to locate a woman whose physical appearance defied those laws was proving how strict and rigid a set of laws those were. As the evening of my dinner with Naomi approached, and as my search for that elusive combination of attractive unprettiness continued to falter, an oppressive combination of anxiety and dread grew within me, until, for better or worse, the time for our date had finally come.

* * *

On purpose, I arrived at the restaurant 15 minutes early. I wanted to see Naomi before she saw me. Not that I was going to bolt if I didn't like what I saw—I would never do that. I just wanted the advantage of those three or four seconds before she saw me to make sure that I could replace any embarrassing look of disappointment with a more neutral expression of friendliness. This was my first real date as an adult—my first blind date ever—and I was determined to

19

handle it like the mature person I presumed myself to be. I was having dinner with this woman, no matter what.

I ordered a drink at the bar, then positioned myself so that I had an unobstructed view of the restaurant's front door. Couples walked in and out intermittently, and then, after ten minutes or so, the door opened, in walked my date, and in that instant I understood exactly what the phrase, "not pretty, but attractive," meant.

The "not pretty" part meant that Naomi was, indeed, "not pretty." Under no known definition of the word, in this or any other language, on this or any other planet, could Naomi be described as pretty. She was, definitively, not pretty. To call her pretty would be lying. It would be making fun of pretty. She was, in fact, ugly. Very ugly.

The "but attractive" part meant this: It meant that she was so ridiculously ugly, she could earn a living as a circus "attraction."

I know that sounds harsh, and to anyone offended by the brutishness of my description, I apologize. I am certainly no Pierce Brosnan, and I'm sure many a woman wouldn't give me a second look. Beauty is in the eye of the beholder, of course, and what might be unappealing to me could very well spark the interest of someone else. In this case, though, the only type of man whose interest would be sparked by a woman who looked like Naomi would be a man with a passion for facial hair.

Needless to say, the date trudged along laboriously. I had committed myself to dinner with Naomi, and I was honoring that commitment to the end, but the shortcomings of her appearance cast an obvious pall on the entire evening. When the waiter, during one of Naomi's bathroom breaks, asked me, in all seriousness, "Do you think your mother would like some more coffee," I knew that I was not the only one to notice her less-than-flattering features. Finally, the check arrived, and after paying the bill, walking Naomi to her car, and kissing her hairy cheek, my first post-marital date came to an end.

I got in my car and immediately called Helen.

"So?" she asked excitedly, "So tell me, how'd it go? What'd she look like?"

"Well," I said, "remember the movie Planet of the Apes?"

"Uh, yea," she said.

"And remember that one of the main characters was a female scientist ape?"

"Oh no," Helen said, "Don't tell me . . ."

"Well," I said, "imagine that the female scientist ape had an ugly sister."

Helen groaned sympathetically. "Oh, Kenny, I am so, so sorry. I was afraid that would happen."

What? What did she just say?

"What do you mean you were afraid that would happen?" I asked. "Did you know that this woman looked like John Belushi, but with more fur?"

"No," Helen said, "but when I called Robin that night to find out about the blonde hair-brown hair thing, she said something that made me worry about this date."

"Yeah, I know, you told me—the thing about her not being pretty, but that she was attractive."

"No," Helen said, "she said something else that made me think you might not like Naomi."

"And what was that?" I asked.

"Well," Helen said, "I think she said something like, 'Oh, he's definitely not going to like Naomi.'"

I pulled the cell phone away from my ear and stared at it, not quite believing what I was hearing.

"Do you mean to say," I asked, "that after finding out you'd given me the wrong number, you then found out that the woman whose number you did give me was someone I was *definitely* not going to like, and yet you didn't tell me that? You let me go out on a date with someone you knew would not appeal to me? How could you do that?"

Helen paused.

"Well," she finally said, "I just figured, hey, what the hell—you never know."

CHAPTER TWO—MORE THAN A HUNDRED

I suppose I learned a few things from the Naomi debacle. For one thing, I learned that I prefer women with less facial hair than I. That was important. I learned that the laws of mathematics are, indeed, inviolate, and that a great conversation on the phone is no predictor of physical attraction. I learned not to obsess so much about when to call and what to say—instead, just pick up the phone, dial the number, and let the dynamics take over—although, when given a number to call, I learned to make sure it belongs to the originally intended callee. Still, my response to Helen's cavalierly fatalistic, "You never know," was to tell her that her matchmaking license—at least with respect to me—was revoked.

"Helen," I told her, "from this point forward, you *do* know. You're my friend, and I love you, but you are to matchmaking what Robitussin is to winemaking, so please don't try to set me up again."

Not only had she bungled the setup of the first blind date of my life, she even ruined any opportunity I might have had to meet the originally intended "really, really cute" woman. It seems Naomi, as Robin's friend, was also friendly with the blonde legal secretary, and Robin, Helen and I all felt that trying to set me up with the blonde immediately after my date with Naomi would be, shall we say, indelicate, to say the least.

I was, therefore, more than a bit skeptical when Helen's 22-year-old daughter, Lainie, called a few weeks later to tell me about someone she knew who was "just perfect" for me.

"Lainie," I said, "if it's someone in your age bracket she's way too young, and if you're acting as a front for your mother, well, tell her I'm not that easily fooled."

"No," Lainie protested, "she's not one of my friends, and my mother has nothing to do with this, I swear! Her name is Vicki, and she's a stylist at the place where I get my hair cut. She's 39 years old, never been married, has a great sense of humor, is a lot of fun, and she's very pretty, Kenny, I mean it, very pretty!"

I asked the obvious question: "If she's that great, how come she's never been married?"

It's a reasonable question, borne of the undeniable sociological truth of living in modern-day America. While the trends have been inching upwards of late, the numbers still show that in this country, most middle class men and women tend to marry and start families between the ages of 25 and 35, and so, while finding single, never-married people in their late 30s or early 40s is not necessarily rare, it is outside the norm. Finding single, never-married people in that age bracket who are also well-adjusted, good-looking, with great senses of humor—and no "issues" scaring them away from intimacy or commitment—is harder still.

"I have no idea, Kenny, I'm not her shrink," Lainie said, "all I know is that she's a really great girl, very pretty, and I think you'd really like her. And I have much better taste than my mother. Trust me."

Part of me was inclined to take a pass. Being set up by a 22-year-old child of a friend of mine, even though she was trying to introduce me to a woman who was 39, was odd enough, but I will also confess to a certain amount of unfair, immature snobbishness about going out with a hairdresser. I mean, here I was, a professional with a graduate degree— shouldn't I be dating other professionals? Would I really have anything in common with a hairdresser? Could such a match possibly work?

On the other hand, didn't Barbra Streisand go out with her hairdresser for years, and didn't he end up running some movie studio or something? I had always tried to live my life without prejudging people, and yet wasn't my knee-jerk assumption of incompatibility with a hairdresser—especially one I'd not yet met—just another example of rank bigotry? Besides, didn't Lainie say that Vicki was very pretty?

I wavered for a few seconds as I wrestled with my thoughts, but ultimately succumbed to "very pretty."

"Okay, Lainie," I said, "give me her number. I'll call her."

* * *

Very pretty. What is it about "very pretty" that can make a man drop his defenses? Certainly, Lainie said several flattering things about Vicki—a great sense of humor, a lot of fun, a great girl—but without the "very pretty," I doubt I would have relented. I'm not proud of how shallow that sounds, but, shallow or not, it's true. While "pretty," on its own, might not be enough to sustain a long-term, meaningful relationship, as an initial enticer "pretty" is pretty much the champion.

* * *

Having learned from the Naomi episode not to obsess about the call, I didn't even put the phone down after hanging up with Lainie. Instead, I dialed Vicki's number then and there, and after two rings she answered the phone.

"Hello, Vicki?"

"Yes."

"Hi, Vicki, this is Kenn Shapiro. I just got off the phone with our mutual acquaintance, Lainie, who said such flattering things about you that I decided to call you immediately, before some other, more desirable man steals you away."

Smooth, eh?

In retrospect, that opening seems so smarmy, almost tacky, and certainly too smooth for the rookie that I was at the time. It was, however, spontaneous—calling without a plan was clearly the way to go for me. More importantly, it worked. Vicki laughed, then responded with some appropriately modest remark about how Lainie had obviously exaggerated, and for the next 45 minutes we kidded and chatted and bantered about in a free-flowing, lighthearted repartee which ended with me suggesting, and Vicki eagerly assenting, that we meet for drinks and dinner later in the week.

* * *

This time, the period between phone call and date was not nearly as nerve-wracking. For one thing, while it's true that this was only the second blind date of my life, having that first one under my belt helped diminish the anxiety that often accompanies first-time experiences. More importantly, on this date, the person I'd be meeting would actually be the woman the fixer-upper intended me to meet, and while there was no guarantee that my taste would coincide with Lainie's, I was far less apprehensive about meeting a woman described as "very pretty" than I was about meeting one whose description was somewhat less easily comprehended.

Once again, I arrived at the restaurant early. This would become, I decided, part of my first date protocol. Being comfortably ensconced on a bar stool substantially reduced the potential for an embarrassing misstep during that instant of first eye contact—I didn't have to worry about tripping over something, I didn't have to think about whether to walk with my hands in my pockets or at my side, and I didn't have to fret about looking like a simp as I scanned the room searching for a face I'd never before seen. Instead, I could assuage at least some of my jitters and insecurities, and maybe even pass myself off as confident and relaxed, by sitting at the bar, watching the front door, and making initial eye contact without having to concentrate on any other basic motor skill.

A few minutes later—with me sitting stiffly at the bar, eyes glued to the door, but comfortable with the deluded notion that my affect was all casual and light—Vicki walked in. At about 5' 3", maybe 110 pounds, she was petite, trim, and shapely—all good things. She was also pretty. So far, Lainie was on the mark. From ten feet away, she saw me, smiled (which had to be a good sign), then cocked her head as if to say, without words, "Is it you?"

I nodded, she approached, and I put out my hand.
"Vicki?"
"Kenn?"
As she took my hand, we were both smiling. This was getting off to a very good start. She had dark hair, and was wearing a black top, but her eyes—her best feature—were a light shade of green, and the contrast was striking. Her perfume was strong—probably a bit too strong—but her overall manner was so pleasing, and she came across instantly as so relaxed, that I decided it really didn't matter. She ordered a glass of wine, I nursed the scotch I'd been drinking since before she arrived, and by the time we finished our first round the table was ready and it was time to move into the

dining room. Wow, I thought—I'm having a good time! And so is she!

We talked non-stop. She talked, I listened. I talked, she listened. We laughed. I asked questions, she asked questions, and we each seemed genuinely interested in learning about the other. As the evening progressed, though, Vicki seemed to take the lead, revealing facts and moments and milestones that were more private than I'd expected to hear on a first date. Gradually but steadily, her revelations took on an air of intimacy, as if, with each bit of self-disclosure, she was slowly peeling away layers of protection, layers of armor, layers of clothing, opening herself up to scrutiny, with all the potential for pleasure and pain that naturally follows. I learned during appetizers that while she was very close to her mother, she hadn't spoken to her father in 17 years, and didn't know whether he was dead or alive. I learned during the main course that she'd had a seven-year romance and a four-year romance, but, regrettably, neither turned out to be the love of her life. I learned just before dessert that she'd lost her virginity at 17, while in high school, to a college boy who told her he loved her, then never called her again. With each new revelation, the conversation turned to matters more private, more intimate, and there seemed to be no barrier, no limit, no topic that was out of bounds. While a part of me was embarrassed by the sensitive nature of her disclosures—it felt almost voyeuristic to learn these things so early in the process of getting to know someone—I reminded myself that I'd been living in the cocoon of marriage for the past 17 years, and that perhaps this was not unusual in the world of middle-aged dating. Still, I was surprised, and a bit taken aback, when she turned to me as the waiter was pouring our coffee and asked, "So, Kenny, tell me: How many woman have you been with?"

* * *

I demurred at first, trying to sound gallant and discrete. "Oh, come on," I said, "you don't want to know the answer to that question." Vicki had revealed a lot about herself, but this, it seemed to me, was pushing the envelope.

"No—I do!" she said, "Really, I do. Tell me. How many?"

I resisted again, but she would not relent.

"Really," she said, "it's okay. Just tell me. I really want to know."

I was conflicted. Yes, I was new to the dating world, and I certainly had a lot to learn about the do's and the don'ts and the overall social norms and niceties of the process—but, newcomer or not, telling a woman, on a first date, about all the other women you've had sex with just had to be on everybody's list of "What Not To Do." On the other hand, Vicki had been so unabashedly and unexpectedly forthcoming, so open and honest, that it hardly seemed fair for me not to respond in kind.

"I don't know about this, Vicki," I said, "I mean, are you sure you want to cover this territory?"

"I'm sure," she said playfully. "I can take it. Hit me with your best shot."

"All right," I said, then I put my head back to do a count. It hadn't been that many—I'd been married for 17 mostly faithful years, and there were just a few women before my marriage—but, still, I wanted to give her an accurate number, so after running through the names in my head and making sure I hadn't left anyone out, I gave her the final tally. (It was a number I'll not repeat here, other than to say that it was respectable, but not slutty.)

29

"Hmm," she murmured, seeming neither offended nor impressed—just genuinely interested. And so, without skipping a beat, I looked across the table and asked, "And you?"

She seemed surprised. "And me, what?"

"Oh, come on now" I said, smiling. "You know what I'm asking. You asked me, now I'm asking you: How many men have you been with?"

"Oh, God," she insisted, "I can't answer that question."

"Of course you can," I said, "I answered your question, now you can answer mine. What's the problem?"

She hesitated, then said, "I just don't feel comfortable answering that question, that's all."

"Look, Vicki," I said, "I'm no psychologist, but I know enough about human nature to know that the only reason you would ask me, on our first date, to tell you about how many woman I'd slept with, is because you wanted me to ask you about your sexual history, so here we are—I'm giving you the opportunity to tell me. I know you've been single, and you're an attractive, engaging woman, so there have undoubtedly been men in your life. I'm a grown-up. I can handle it. Tell me. I'm prepared."

I had in my mind the scene from the movie, "Four Weddings and a Funeral," where Andie McDowell is telling Hugh Grant about all the men she's slept with. She goes through the first eight or nine and he nods politely as she briefly describes each one. Then, as she talks about number ten, then number sixteen, then twenty-two, his face starts gradually to wilt as his facade of bravado and nonchalance gives way to the jealousy and unease he's been trying to suppress, until, finally, as she finishes somewhere in the 20's or 30's, you see in his expression a mixture of discomfort and relief as the torturous parade comes to a finish.

"You really want to know?" Vicki asked.

"It's not so much that I want to know," I said, "but that I know you want to tell me. So," I continued, as I conjured up the image of Grant and McDowell and prepared myself for the inevitable list of the twenty or thirty men from her past, "go ahead and tell me how many men you've been with. I'm prepared."

"Well," she said, then lifted up her coffee cup, took a sip slowly, put the cup down, swallowed the coffee, looked at me for a second or two, then finally continued:

"More than a hundred . . . ."

* * *

You know, the brain is a funny thing. There were two parts to her answer, with the second part coming barely half a second after the first, separated by nothing more than the equivalent of a comma in the middle of a sentence, but in that brief instant—in the fraction of a second it took to place that figurative comma between the two parts of the answer—my brain processed dozens of thoughts. After hearing the first part, the "more than a hundred" part, but before hearing the rest of the sentence—indeed, before Vicki even began to utter the rest of the sentence, and before my face had received enough synaptic signals to begin a responsive expression—my mind raced: What?! More than a hundred?! My God! Is she kidding?! Am I catching something just by sitting here?! I could probably have sex with her tonight! Do I want to have sex with her tonight? Or ever? She's probably a sex animal! Do I have enough condoms? Do I have any condoms with disinfectant? And on and on.

Clearly, I was not prepared for her answer. This was not the way it happened in the movie. More than a hundred?! Then, in the midst of the dozens of not-yet-fully-processed thoughts—after the bare blink of an eye in real time—Vicki completed her sentence:

". . . but I've decided to give up sex forever."

* * *

"More than a hundred, but I've decided to give up sex forever."

* * *

So that was her answer. She's slept with over one hundred men, but has now decided—and has told me during the dessert portion of an otherwise thoroughly enjoyable date—to give up sex forever. Despite the frenetic ruminations still bouncing their way around my brain, I managed to remain outwardly composed, nonplussed even, as though what I'd just heard wasn't all that unexpected or outrageous. I nodded my head, lifted my cup of coffee, and, just before taking a sip, said, simply, "Yes, well, I suppose that's one approach."

We tried to make small talk for the next five minutes or so, but while I saw Vicki's lips moving, I wasn't hearing a thing. The evening had obviously taken an abrupt left turn, and I was not optimistic about a course correction anytime soon. Finally, after a brief but awkward silence, and with not much at that point to lose, I decided to revisit the subject.

"Vicki," I said, "I've been thinking about what we were talking about a few minutes ago, you know, about the number of guys you've been with and the giving up sex and all that, and there's a question I have that's been bothering me."

She was clearly uncomfortable, but she nodded so I continued.

"Well," I said, "here's the question. You're 39 years old, and you told me you lost your virginity when you were 17, so that would leave 22 years of sexual activity. You also told me about a seven year exclusive relationship and a four year exclusive relationship, so that takes 11 years out of the 22, leaving 11 years of non-exclusive sexual activity. You said you were with more than a hundred guys, so I'm going to assume, say, roughly one-fifty. A hundred and fifty men during a period of 11 years comes out to about one different guy each and every month for 11 years, which is a fairly active sex life. And we're here tonight having drinks and dinner, so you're obviously still dating. So my question—which I'm asking only because I'm new to this dating thing, and I want to be sure I'm not making some ridiculously obvious blunders as I lumber my way through this process—is this: Was your decision to give up sex forever a decision you made before tonight, or does it have something to do with me?"

Her face devolved into a look of anger and disgust as she grabbed her purse and stood to leave.

"I knew it," she growled, "you're all the same. You just don't fucking get it, do you? You just don't understand. Go fuck yourself, okay?"

Then she left.

I don't know—I thought it was a reasonable question.

CHAPTER THREE—A BLACK PRINT DRESS

Okay, so maybe I hadn't found romance on either of my first two post-marital dates, but I was getting an education. As with the Naomi experience, I picked up a lesson or two from my drinks and dinner with Vicki. I learned that when a woman on a first date reveals sensitive intimacies very quickly, it could be because you're just one of those men to whom women feel comfortable opening up, or it might be because the chemistry is so potent she feels as though she's known you forever—more likely, though, it's because she simply gives the goods away too easily. I learned to pay special attention the next time a woman says she hasn't spoken to her father in years—again, I'm no psychologist, but there must have been some connection between Vicki's shattered relationship with her father and her insatiable appetite for men. And I learned that maybe I should be wary of too much perfume—perhaps its purpose is to try to mask something. Whatever.

I also learned never to accept another fix-up from any member of Helen's family. Which is why, when Jodi Adams called me at work three weeks later offering to set me up with a friend of hers, my first question was, "Are you related by blood or marriage to Helen Eisenberg?" As I suspected, Jodi—a client of mine who worked in the same building as I—had never heard of Helen.

"Okay," I said. "I'll listen."

Jodi ran a public relations firm, and so, as you might expect, she knew a lot of people—and she liked to talk. She had used this combination to build a fairly successful **PR** business, but she'd also used it to develop an avocation as a matchmaker. When word circled around to her that I had started dating, she wasted no time trying to add me to her short but, in her words, "extraordinary" list of successful love matches.

"I don't know what it is about me, Kenny," she gushed, as only a good PR operative could gush, "but I have some kind of talent, some sixth sense, that enables me to put the right people together with each other, and, I'm telling you, I have the right person for you."

Why do some people say "I'm telling you" when they're telling you something? I mean, isn't it obvious?

She continued like one long trumpet note, without taking a breath: "She's 40 years old, divorced, but with no kids, which is great, don't you think, 'cause like it's no baggage, you know what I mean? And she's really bright, and she has her own business, so that's great, too, 'cause like she's not looking for anyone to support her or anything, you know? She lives in New York, but she comes to Florida all the time for business, and there's no reason she couldn't live here in Florida because her business involves national sales, and so it doesn't really matter where she lives, and I know she would move here if she met the right person, and I think you are definitely the right person."

As I said—she could talk.

"Jodi," I said, "slow down. I'm not interested in dating anyone who lives in New York, and I'm certainly not ready for the responsibility of having someone move down to Florida just to be with me—I'm not even legally divorced yet, for crying out loud." The final papers were still weeks away from being signed.

"Listen," she said, shifting gears to a softer sell, "I know all that, but you'd really like her, I just know it, and she's coming down to Fort Lauderdale next weekend for business, so she'll be down here anyway, and so why not go out with her just to have a night out? What's the harm in that?"

I knew what Jodi was doing—she was so sure I'd like her friend, so sure we'd end up on her "extraordinary" list of successful love matches, that she'd use any pitch available as long as the end result found me meeting this woman face-to-face. I could see through her transparent ploy.

Ploy or not, though, there was a certain harmless logic to her position. I mean, no law says each date has to have as its ultimate purpose the eventual pairing-up of its participants—some dates can be had and enjoyed for the sole purpose of spending a night out with someone new, can't they? And, viewed that way, what really would be the harm in agreeing to a night on the town with Jodi's baggage-free friend from New York?

I was beginning to soften.

"What does she look like?" I asked.

* * *

Do blind people ever ask that question? Why are good looks such an important determinant of whether one is willing to be set up with a stranger? Are good-looking people, empirically, better mates in the long run? Are they kinder? Are they better kissers? Better lovers? Better parents?

Although I've never studied the issue, I think it's probably safe to say that the comeliness of a person's appearance bears no relation whatsoever to whether that person's character, values, personality, or desires will be compatible over the long term with those of the person who initially admires the good looks. I think it's probably also safe to say that most of us have known people whom we did not initially consider to be visually appealing, but who became so over time not because of any physical changes in appearance, but because of our gradually increasing appreciation for the totality of their personas.

So why are good looks so initially important in the context of a blind date?

I don't know. But they are.

* * *

"She's very cute, Kenny, and smart, and successful, and really personable. You've got nothing to lose. I mean, you've got to eat anyway, right? You're gonna have dinner next weekend regardless, right? So why not have that dinner with her, and see what happens? It's just one date."

Jodi was right. Even if nothing came of it—and surely nothing would—why have dinner alone when I could have dinner with a cute, smart, successful, personable woman?

"Okay," I said, "give me her name and her number. I'll call her tonight."

* * *

Her name was Tracey, and of the three "first call," "break-the-ice" telephone chats I'd had in my brief post-marital dating life, this was by far the most head-swelling. She came right out and said at the outset that she was very eager to meet me, and everything I said after that, no matter how innocuous or self-deprecating, seemed to heighten her desire.

"Jodi said such amazing things about you," she said. "She told me that if she weren't married, she'd be pursuing you herself."

"Well," I said, "let's remember that Jodi is a public relations professional, so she earns her living by promoting, and while I'm sure that all the nice things she's said about you are right on the money, I think you should figure that she's exaggerated just a bit about me."

"Oh, you're just being modest," she said, "but I really like that in a man."

"No, really," I said, "I'm very new to this whole dating thing, and so far I think I've been pretty clumsy about it all, so please don't get your hopes up."

"Oh, you're just trying to lower my expectations," she said, "but it's having the opposite effect."

Wow, I thought, I have no idea what I'm doing, but whatever it is, this cute New Yorker is liking it. This date might be enjoyable after all.

"You know, Kenny," she said, "I'll be staying at the SeaShore Hotel, and I won't have a car with me, so instead of meeting at a restaurant, why don't you come pick me up at the hotel on Friday night?"

"Sure," I said, "I can do that."

"Have you ever stayed at the SeaShore?" she asked. "It's such a romantic hotel."

"Yes," I said, "it's very nice."

"Whenever I stay there," she continued, "I like to order up a bottle of wine at night, then I keep the terrace door open before I crawl into bed so I can fall asleep to the sound of the ocean."

Hmm.

Was I hearing her correctly, or was I letting my imagination run just a bit? Was she mentioning the hotel— and the wine, and the ocean, and how romantic it was—just to make conversation? Or was she, in a not-so-subtle way, trying to suggest that I might be invited to join her? She was, after all, from out of town, and so she, too, might very well be assuming that nothing serious or long-term was likely to result from our casual dinner date—perhaps she was just looking for an uncomplicated, romantic weekend.

This might be a really, really good date.

We agreed that I would pick her up at 7:30, Friday night, in front of the hotel.

"I'll be standing under the canopy by the valet stand," she said, "and I'll be wearing a black print dress."

* * *

I left work early that Friday. I had a feeling about this date, and I wanted enough time to prepare myself completely. At various times throughout my adult life I'd heard stories about situations like this. The stories were always second or third-hand, where someone knew someone who told them about someone else, but they always involved the same theme—two people from different places meet, sparks fly, and without the risk of bumping into each other at the gas station or the dry cleaners or anywhere else a week or two down the road, without the natural hesitation that inhibits people from moving too quickly if they perceive the possibility of a true "relationship," they instead throw caution to the wind and enjoy a torrid weekend of wild romance, parting forever when the weekend ends, content and fulfilled from the pleasure-packed, guiltless experience they each cherish and remember for the rest of their natural lives.

Okay, so perhaps the stories I'd heard had been embellished somewhat as they passed from teller to teller. Still, unless I had badly misread Tracey's signals, this date had the potential for some romance of the physical variety, and I intended to be ready for all contingencies.

First, I went to the gym for a full workout. (For me, a "full workout" consisted of a few sets of reps on some circuit training machines, fifty pushups, and twenty minutes on the treadmill, but the flimsiness of my workout was less important than what it represented, which was my determination to arrive at this date in tip-top shape.) After that I went home for a half-hour of sunning in my backyard, convinced that a New Yorker coming to Florida would expect her Floridian date to be freshly tanned. Then, after showering, shaving, and putting on my gray Calvin Klein briefs and my nicest Friday-evening, dress-casual ensemble, I nervously reached into a bathroom drawer for something I'd purchased just the day before, in anticipation of this evening's date—a brand new box of condoms.

Of course I couldn't take the whole box with me—there were twelve condoms in the box, and even if this date turned into a weekend whirlwind, I would not likely need all twelve of them. I decided, instead, to take three, but I was faced with this dilemma: Where do I put them?

I could leave two in the glove compartment of my car, but not all three—that first one had to be handy, but not obvious, and if I were to reach into the glove compartment to retrieve a condom on our drive back to the hotel after dinner, it might seem presumptuous, if not obnoxious. No, that first one had to be hidden away somewhere on my person, so I could accept her expected invitation to return to her room with the knowledge and the confidence that if matters progressed to the point of ultimate passion, I would not have to run down to the car for a trusty Trojan. There would be time enough later, after our first encounter, for me to excuse myself while I grabbed the two extras from the glove box, but that first time had to happen in a natural flow of escalating heat, and for that to happen properly I had to have that first one close by and accessible. But where?

I was not in the habit of carrying a wallet, so I couldn't hide it in there (that would seem so "high school" anyway). Keeping it in my pocket was out of the question—the tell-tale circular outline might reveal itself through my pants, and that would just look cheesy and awful. As I surveyed myself in the mirror, trying to locate a discretely inconspicuous spot in which to stash my foil-wrapped protection, there it was, both obvious and perfect:

My sock.

With condom number one now safely secured against my right ankle, hidden by my sock and my pant leg, and with condoms two and three tucked comfortably into the glove box, I set out on the half-hour drive from my house to the SeaShore hotel, anxious but optimistic about the evening ahead. Since Tracey would be waiting for me at the valet stand outside the hotel, I'd have to forego my preferred technique of arriving at the meeting place before my date, but since I knew she'd be in a black print dress, and inasmuch as I never told her what type of car I'd be driving, I figured I'd still have a few seconds, as I drove up, to notice her before she saw me.

I was right.

As I pulled into the parking lot of the SeaShore, I could see the hotel entrance and the valet stand up ahead, about thirty yards or so. A long line of cars slowed my approach, but from that distance, sure enough, I could see what appeared to be someone in a black print dress standing next to a large, round, concrete post, about two feet wide. My heartbeat quickened and my palms turned clammy as a wave of nervous anticipation came over me—I've never before met this woman, I thought, but if I've read her hints correctly, and if I play my cards right, I could be sleeping with her in a matter of hours. One by one the line of cars inched forward, until, as the distance shrunk and I was able to differentiate more clearly all the people and objects crowding the valet stand, the reality of what I was looking at came more clearly into view.

The black print dress was unmistakable, and it was the only black print dress among the crowd, so the woman in the dress, clearly, was Tracey. However, the large, round, two-foot-wide concrete post was, in fact, not a concrete post at all—it was, instead, Tracey's left leg.

And it was accompanied—as they most often are—by an equally massive right leg.

* * *

Tracey was enormous. I flirted briefly with the notion of turning the car around and heading home, but the idea was rude and ungentlemanly, and I abandoned it quickly—plus, the way my car was wedged in to the long valet line, there was no physical way of actually turning the thing around. As I finally reached the valet stand, I rolled down the passenger side window and nodded at Tracey, who was looking inquiringly at me.

"Tracey?" I asked through the window.

She smiled broadly and bounded over to the car, almost leaping in as she opened the door.

"Hi, Kenn," she said cheerily as she settled in. "It's so, so nice to meet you!"

"Likewise," I lied, as I shook her hand. "How about we get something to eat?"

"That sounds great to me," she said—and I was sure she wasn't lying.

* * *

Why was I so instantly turned off by Tracey's heft? Was it because I, at 5'7" and 150 pounds, am a relatively slight fellow, and so standing next to Tracey (about 5'5"—in diameter) seemed a bit like Laurel standing next to Hardy? Perhaps. Few men, I think, whatever their sexual preferences, fantasize about Oliver Hardy types, and, for better or worse, I have always had a bias in favor of women who tend toward thin. I think, though, that what irked me more than the emphatic fullness of Tracey's appearance was the fact that the woman who set me up with her—Jodi Adams—thought that Tracey was "just perfect" for me. What did that say about Jodi? Or worse, what did that say about me?

* * *

We drove the short distance to the restaurant, during which time I was able to notice, even though it was dark, that Tracey was not only somewhat bulky, she was also somewhat funny looking. It was not merely that she was unattractive—and she was unattractive—but part of what made her so unattractive (apart from the weight) was that her nose sat just a bit too high on her face, and her mouth sat just a bit too low, resulting in a very large area that, for lack of a better understanding of anatomy, I'll refer to as the mustache area. And while she didn't have a mustache, the wide expanse of that area—the wide expanse of bare skin between the bottom of her nose and the top of her upper lip—resulted in a facial appearance that reminded me of something familiar, something I'd seen before, although at first I couldn't quite place it. Then, as I parked at the restaurant and had the opportunity to look at her face directly, not just from the side, it came to me. Tracey looked uncannily like a Muppet.

As we settled into the restaurant, I had visions of the waiter putting a glass of water on the table next to me, and a bowl of water on the floor next to Tracey. He didn't, but he might as well have. Clearly unconcerned with the Madison Avenue ideal of a fit, trim American woman, Tracey indulged her passion for food with shameless zeal. She tore through the initial basket of baguettes as though they were jelly beans—heavily buttered jelly beans—then cleaned her plate of every morsel of salad, going so far as to suck the leftover dressing off her spoon as if it were soup. She snarfed down her salmon with gusto, then asked for a second basket of baguettes, which she used as edible sponges with which to soak up and consume the leftover dill sauce on her plate—as well as the leftover ginger glaze on mine. As I watched her methodically plowing her way through dessert (a fudge brownie mud pie with two extra scoops of vanilla ice cream), she actually appeared to grow larger before my very eyes. At one point I felt a sensation near my ankle, and I was afraid to look down, fearful that I'd see the condom leaping out of my sock, running toward the door, waving back at me saying, "You're on your own, pal!" She was ravenous. She was insatiable.

She would be spending the night alone.

CHAPTER FOUR—A BETTER WAY

Tracey did, finally, finish her dessert, and by 9:30 that evening I had dropped her off safely at the SeaShore valet stand, politely declining her invitation to see the view from her room. As I pulled away, I saw her saying something to the bellman, and while I couldn't quite hear the conversation word-for-word, I'm pretty sure she was asking whether the snacks portion of her mini-bar had as yet been re-stocked.

* * *

I finessed the Monday morning call from Jodi— "Thanks for the set-up, Jodi, but the chemistry just wasn't there"—but a bigger issue started to gnaw at me. Why was I being set up with women so obviously ill-suited for me? It wasn't just those first few dates. A couple of weeks after my food orgy with Tracey, the wife of another friend called with the phone number of a woman who worked at a local clothing store.

"I think she'd be good for you, Kenny—give her a call."

I called the woman, whose name was Ellen.

"Ellen," I said, winging it, "I've been told you're lovely and adorable, which are two of the four things I look for in a woman."

"Really?" she said. "What are the other three?"

Hmm.

Then there was Audrey, the cousin of another friend. I picked Audrey up at her apartment, and on our way to the restaurant for dinner she asked me to stop at the local drug store, where she proceeded to fill her prescription for NasalCrom, and then, on our way to the checkout counter, and right before my eyes, added a package of Vagisil. I'm sure she had a lot to say during dinner, but I could focus on nothing but the thought of her stuffy nose and her itchy vagina.

What was going on here? Was it really this hard to connect with someone? All during my married life (or so it seemed), I'd encountered smart, pretty, single women, all of whom complained about the dearth of good, eligible men. Where were these women now? And why was no one setting me up with them? Why, instead, was I being set up with unattractive women who ate too much, no longer had sex, flunked math, and had hygiene issues?

There had to be a better way.

* * *

For months, I dated no one. Friends were running out of fix-up possibilities, and I'd grown so gun-shy that what few offers I'd received, I turned down. I lived in a suburban environment that was great for my kids—lots of parks, great schools, very family-oriented neighborhoods—but it might as well have been Siberia for a single person. My law practice rarely took me out of my office, so I almost never came across single women through my work. And although my divorce had been finalized, my ex became ill shortly thereafter, so my leisure and charitable pursuits—which might have afforded me the opportunity for a love connection here or there—gave way to the more immediate and important responsibilities of raising my two adolescent children. All of these factors combined more or less to put me into a state of romantic hibernation.

Against this backdrop, one night during the Spring of 1999, my 12-year-old daughter called out to me from her bedroom.

"Daddy," she said, as I heard her giggling from down the hall, "you've got to see this!"

She was at her computer, looking at a web page she'd found on America Online. Her Bat Mitzvah was still several months away, but she'd been trying to find a theme for the short speech she'd have to give at the synagogue on that special day, and so she'd plugged in the keyword "Jewish" and up came a website entitled something like, "Jewish Community Page." The site had various links to different locations involving an array of Jewish topics, but one of the links was labeled, "Matchmaker." My daughter had clicked onto that link, and in so doing had stumbled across what appeared to both of us to be some type of online dating service.

By today's standards the site was very primitive, but it was the first online dating system I'd ever encountered, and I was dumbfounded. I'd heard about some newspapers having online "personals" sections, and even about a few full-fledged online dating services, but my mindframe at the time was that only losers or perverts tried to find romance on the Internet. The notion of participating in such an activity—of revealing one's singleness to the entire world by posting a picture and a profile in cyberspace, where people you didn't even know might be making judgments about you without your knowledge—seemed patently ridiculous to me. I was stunned, therefore, to find that the supposedly serious-minded people who'd set up the "Jewish Community Page" on America Online had apparently created and endorsed just such an activity.

Arranged by state, by age, and by gender were hundreds upon hundreds of individual profiles, each with a photograph, in which men and women shamelessly offered self-details (body type, height, eye color, occupation, number of children) alongside brief essays in which they described themselves and the characteristics they sought in a mate.

One by one, I browsed through the profiles, shaking my head and smirking over the embarrassment of it all. Women in glamour shots, women in bikinis, writing about how they liked bungee jumping, and hang-gliding, and walks on the beach. Businessmen in business suits, bare-chested men in bathing suits, writing about how they liked football and scuba diving and, of course, walks on the beach. It all seemed so tacky and so desperate.

It also seemed so naked. To my thinking, the ordinary progression of romantic human interaction began with some type of contact between two specific people—a meeting, a phone call, maybe just an exchange of letters—followed by a gradual progression of innocuous self-disclosure, then more intimate self-disclosure, then perhaps, with the right chemistry, a move toward physical intimacy and, with any luck, couplehood. Such a progression had layers—clothing, if you will—which peeled away in relation to the level of familiarity and comfort the two specific people achieved with one another. Sometimes achieving that level took weeks or months, sometimes it took mere hours, but the steps to that level usually followed a predictable A to B to C path.

This was different. As I clicked through profile after profile on the Matchmaker web site, I could not help feeling like a voyeur, feeling as though I were looking at people who had removed a layer or two of clothing and displayed the results for anyone to see, all in a calculated compromise between dignity and desire. It was discomforting. It was sad.

It was also very entertaining.

* * *

For the next month or two, with increasing frequency, I'd find myself logging on to the Matchmaker web site, not in a hunt for romance, but as an incredulous spectator of this revealing phenomenon. Each time, as I'd pull up listing after listing of women declaring how equally comfortable they were in evening gowns as in jeans, or how little the location of a date mattered as long as they enjoyed the company of the man they were with, I'd shake my head, not believing how mercantile and impersonal it all seemed—complex human beings willingly reduced to billboard versions of themselves, all in a hungry quest to sell the notion of their love-worthiness. The pathology of it all was deep and fascinating, as engrossing as any good novel, and as with any gripping page-turner, the more I read the less able I was to pull myself away. This was entertainment of the highest order—it had ethos and pathos, comedy and tragedy, all playing out within a setting undeniably pregnant with the prospect of sex and romance.

Pass me the popcorn!

Then, one lonely Saturday night in early July of that year, while clicking through the profiles of women in Ohio, a page came up that surprised me. The woman's picture was very pretty, but that was not unusual—the site had many pretty pictures. What surprised me about this particular profile, as I began to read through the woman's brief essay, was this:

It seemed honest.

That's not to say that the hundreds of earlier profiles I'd read were dishonest. "Dishonest" suggests deceit, or a conscious effort to mislead, and I don't believe that the vast majority of people revealing themselves on the Matchmaker website had any desire purposely to fool anyone. But, to this point in my journey through the postings of single women—a journey that had thus far taken me alphabetically through every state from Alabama to Ohio—it seemed as though, in describing themselves, most of the women were describing the person they wished they were, rather than the person they really were. The writing read like advertising, mostly sunny and light—"I'm a fit, fun, attractive mom, and my friends say I'm always smiling" or "I like evenings out on the town, but also snuggling on the couch"—which afforded little insight into the person's heart and soul. But the profile that popped up in front of me, that lonesome night in July, was different.

She didn't quite know what she was looking for, the woman wrote, but she supposed she'd know it when she found it.

Hmm, I thought, this is interesting.

Her name, according to the profile, was Nora. She was 42 (my age at the time), a freelance photographer (a long-neglected hobby of mine), with three adolescent children (one more than I, but I could certainly relate). Her picture had her sitting alone on a field of grass, Indian style, in black jeans and a blue denim button-down shirt, with black sneakers, white socks, blue eyes, dark hair, and an unforced, natural smile—a smile that appeared to be caught *by* the camera, rather than posed *for* the camera.

"I guess," she wrote, "that I'm just hoping to fall in love again, and I'm hoping to be loved, too."

Wow, I thought—that's it. She's nailed it. While everyone else seemed to be trying to make a sale with their various descriptions of moonlit nights and exotic vacations, this woman seemed hardly to be selling at all. She seemed, instead, to be writing from the heart, and with the help of a mere handful of words she stepped out from behind all the self-promoting pitches and packaging that had characterized each of the hundreds of other profiles I'd perused.

This, I said to myself, is a very interesting woman.

* * *

I continued, that night, sifting through the rest of the listings of Ohio women, but after each successive profile, I'd find myself returning to Nora's. The gentle smile, the few threads of commonality between us, her unaffected words—all kept pulling me back. Until now, the silly superficiality of virtually every listing I'd read made it easy for me to be snooty and judgmental about the online dating world and all its inhabitants. Until now, I'd snobbishly concluded that only a shallow desperation or an unhealthy neediness would render someone shameless enough to endure the ignominy of sending a "Someone Please Love Me" postcard to the world. Was Nora's profile—an earnest expression of hope and desire that seemed neither desperate nor needy, neither shallow nor unhealthy—the exception that proved my rule? Or, was it possible that my superior attitude about finding romance online was simply bigoted and hypercritical? Had I been just plain wrong?

In Nora's case, it didn't really matter. After all, she lived in Ohio and I lived in South Florida, so obviously, if love were in fact findable on the Internet (still a very big "if" in my mind), I would not be finding it with Nora. Long distance relationships make good fodder for movies and books, but they seldom succeed in the real world. The blooming of a healthy, sustainable love requires an element of geographic proximity (right?), and Ohio and South Florida were hardly proximate, so any fleeting musings I might have had were purely academic—I would not be starting a romance with Nora. Still, even though a relationship of any kind was out of the question with a woman who lived 1500 miles away, each of the Matchmaker profiles contained its subject's screen name, so communicating via e-mail with Nora, if I were so inclined, would be not only possible, it would be easy.

But should I? I mean, what would be the point?

No point. There would be no point at all in writing to this woman. While it was true that her brief and simple sentences struck a chord in me, and while I couldn't deny being affected by the natural look that came through in her photo, the fact was that this woman exposed herself the way she did only as part of an implicit bargain in which she sought, in exchange, a human connection that might lead to a mutual love. It would therefore be wrong and unfair for me to write to her, since even if I could get past my bias against the whole cyber-process in general, geography would prevent me from offering the second half of the bargain.

On the other hand, what would be the harm in sending this woman a simple note, not with the aim of romance, but just to let her know that an objective observer, one who had no hidden agenda, was moved by the depth and the honesty of her profile? Wouldn't she—wouldn't anyone—be pleased to receive recognition and praise from someone who sought nothing in return, someone whose sole motivation was just a desire to express an appreciation for quality?

After far more equivocating than the import of the decision justified, I stopped thinking and started writing:

Dear Nora:

I'm writing to you from South Florida, so please understand that this e-mail is written with neither the hope nor the expectation of romance. I'm writing instead simply to let you know that I was moved by the honesty of your profile. In a few short sentences, you seemed to open your heart, and in so doing you revealed quite a bit more about yourself—all good. I hope you find what you're looking for, and I hope you didn't mind this brief note. My sole aim was to let you know, for whatever it's worth, that some guy down here in South Florida happened upon your profile, read it, and got it—all of it.

Best of luck to you,
Kenny

After hitting the "send" button, I leaned back, surprisingly satisfied, convinced that at the worst, this anonymous Nora would dismiss me as a meddling interloper (in which case, so what?), and at best, I'd bring a no-cost smile to her face. The last thing I expected from someone so apparently lovely and so undeniably far away was any kind of response.

I was, therefore, surprised the next morning when I logged on to AOL to hear that familiar, "You've got mail," and to see that the e-mail was from Nora.

"Dear Kenny," she wrote:

Thank you so much for your very sweet e-mail. I've received literally hundreds of letters since posting my profile on Matchmaker, but of all the letters I've received, yours was the nicest. What a shame you live so far away! But can you do me a favor? Can you please send me a picture, just so I can put a face to your beautiful words?

Nora

Um—gulp.

This was certainly unexpected. I mean, okay, sure, I probably should have anticipated a thank you from someone as genuine and decent as Nora seemed to be—but a request for my picture? That, it seemed to me, went just a bit further than a mere thank you. What could she possibly want with my picture? Remember, this is the summer of 1999—practically an eon ago in the rapid evolution of the Internet. I had never before sent my picture into cyberspace. What if it ended up all digitized and pixilated atop some camel on a porn site somewhere? I have kids, for crying out loud, and a career. I can't see my life ruined by having my picture float around the world wide web, my likeness hijacked by any two-bit scammer with a working knowledge of digital photo technology. Is she serious? Send her my picture?

On the other hand, maybe she had no ulterior motive. Maybe she really, truly, just wanted to see the face of the person who wrote what she claimed was the nicest e-mail she'd received so far. If, in fact, she actually was the compassionate and thoughtful person I perceived her to be—and the sweetness of her response clearly reinforced that perception—then maybe there was nothing more to her request than what she actually wrote: A desire to put a face to my words.

Oh, I thought, what the hell! All indications are that she's as decent and genuine as I'm presuming her to be—and anyway, who in their right mind would want to paste my ordinary face onto some sex photo—so why not?

I found a somewhat recent picture, cropped it, scanned it, and e-mailed it off to Nora with a brief note, thanking her for taking the time to respond to my previous letter, and wishing her "only the best."

Within hours, she responded yet again:

> Wow—you write beautifully, and you're
> cute, too! Again, what a shame you live
> so far away.

Smiling, I thought to myself, "Well, that was certainly very nice," but as far as I was concerned, that was that—I had written a note designed solely to acknowledge (from afar) her refreshing authenticity, and she'd responded with a thank you and a request. I then responded to her request, and she acknowledged my response. That was it. Mission accomplished. The end. Nora would now continue her search for computer romance in Ohio, and I would continue to entertain myself by rummaging through profiles from my keyboard perch in South Florida. My communication cycle with Nora was complete, and my involvement with her—such as it was—was now over.

Or so I thought.

Three nights later (a Saturday night), while working my way through the profiles of the few Jewish women in South Dakota, I heard a "bling" from my computer and saw a box pop up with a message inside. I had never before received an "Instant Message," and at first it startled me, but I quickly figured out what was happening. It was Nora, and she was writing to me in real time. The message asked:

> What are you doing home on a
> Saturday night?

Obviously, she'd added my screen name to her "Buddy List," and she could see that I was online. I responded:

> Me? I'm just a divorced guy with no life
> and no prospects. Where else would I
> be on a Saturday night? You, on the
> other hand, are a beautiful woman with
> hundreds of men responding to your
> unusually forthright profile, so you have
> no excuse. What are you doing home?

For the initial few minutes, we parried back and forth—playfully at first, perhaps even a bit flirtatiously—but in no time at all this electronic conversation with a faraway stranger turned, remarkably and inexplicably, into a comfortable, unguarded, revelatory exchange. It was odd— but odd in a good way. For all intents and purposes, this woman was alien to me. We'd never met, never spoken, never seen each other in person. My knowledge of her was limited to a few facts, a photograph, a couple of paragraphs of descriptive prose, and an ever-so-brief exchange of electronic correspondence; her knowledge of me was even less. Had we met at a party, or through a fix-up, or through some other, more traditional means, our first snippets of conversation would no doubt have been stilted and nervous and awkward. And yet, here we were, sitting in two separate homes more than a thousand miles away, and in under an hour of typing and sending we'd achieved, with ease, a level of self-disclosure that often takes weeks when the communication line runs face-to-face. It was as if the distance and the anonymity had disarmed our defenses, lowering the walls we all usually employ to protect ourselves from revealing too much too quickly to someone whose presence is new.

After an hour of e-mailing—a dialogue characterized by a steadily increasing level of comfort and familiarity—I finally wrote, "This is silly—what's your phone number?" Two minutes later, we were on the phone, Nora's voice as soft and as feminine as I'd imagined it to be, like the sound of a smile. The obvious wavelength we'd shared in our instant messaging carried over into our telephone conversation, so that by the time one of us had even thought to take a look at a clock, four-and-a-half hours had passed.

The next weekend I was in Ohio.

* * *

Long distance love affairs are, by their nature, bi-polar. When you're with your long-distance lover, it's the equivalent of being on vacation—you've either flown somewhere to be with her, or she's flown somewhere to be with you; you've usually cleared your schedule of work and kids, and she's usually done the same; because your time together is limited, it often involves carefully planned romantic outings or special events, and every night in bed is marked by passion and closeness and the urgency that comes with knowing that the nights are numbered and that they're few and far between. Every moment is a stolen moment, and they all pass too quickly.

When you're away from your long-distance lover, it's hell—extended phone calls filled with longing and frustration; lonely mornings wishing she were there, sharing coffee and conversation over the daily headlines; empty weekends imagining how contented you'd feel if only she were joining you for a movie or accompanying you to that friend's party; the irrational jealousy every time she doesn't answer her phone, as you wonder whether she's out with someone else, someone who lives closer, someone whose proximity gives him the advantage of ready availability. Every moment is a yearning moment, and they all pass too slowly.

Anyway, that's what I learned from my four-month relationship with Nora. All told, we spent perhaps five or six weekends with each other, each filled with the magic and the special intimacy that fuel a burgeoning romance, but each also bookended by torturous weeks of separation. From the outset, the relationship had no realistic potential for an enduring lifespan. Nora had three teenaged children and, understandably, would never have considered disrupting their lives by moving to South Florida, and with two teenaged children, an ailing ex-wife, and a local law practice, I certainly couldn't consider moving to Ohio. We tried, for a while, to deny the existence of the elephant in the room—the elephant that separated South Florida from Ohio—but inevitably the elephant prevailed. We parted ways, painfully, but with each of us determined to try to find someone equally compatible but more geographically accessible. For that brief moment in time, though, the undeniably temporary nature of our relationship mattered less than what the relationship symbolized. For the first time in my post-divorce life, I'd met someone who appealed to me on every level, someone whose presence made me feel a desire to connect, whose softness and gentle manner drew me close. Abbreviated though it was, my relationship with Nora aroused in me the nascent stirrings of love, and left me with the hope that a post-divorce love was, indeed, findable.

And now I knew where to look for it.

CHAPTER FIVE—BUT FIRST, NOT ENOUGH

My time with Nora taught me that even in your forties, a bite from the love bug could make you feel 17 all over again. In the same way that a song or a smell can transport you to your childhood, any post-adolescent infatuation—even one occurring in middle age—is a remembrance of that very first time, and it brings forth from your mind's crusty recesses all those uncorrupted teenage sensations of a first love filled with hope and silliness and promise.

My few months with Nora had all of that. Yes, the lows were awful—the longing that plagued the time between our visits, the visceral ache that would keep me up at night as I'd imagine and crave the comfort and the softness of having her next to me—but those lows were a function of distance more than anything else. If I could find the same connection with someone closer, someone who lived nearby, then I should be able to avoid those long-distance lows and, with any luck, maybe nurture an infatuation into something fuller.

Until now, I didn't know where to look, captive as I was to the tastes, whims, and connections of all those friends and acquaintances with "perfect" fix-ups (who had so far been anything but). Now, though, I knew that not only could I actually find someone worthy and normal on the Internet, I could do it from the comfort of my own home. No need to go trolling in bars, no need to loiter in the produce section of the supermarket, no need to rely on "a friend of a friend who has a friend"—with membership in a couple of Internet dating sites, I could browse through pictures and profiles at my leisure, and, with any luck, find a woman not merely as lovely and compatible as Nora, but local, too. With the Internet dating phenomenon growing exponentially day by day, how hard could such a quest be?

After a small amount of research and a bit of asking around, I identified two particular dating sites that seemed to be the most popular. I was all set to join both, and to begin in earnest my search through the world of cyber romance, but I had one piece of business to take care of beforehand.

At about the beginning of my relationship with Nora, a client of mine started dating a woman with whom he had become instantly smitten. A few weeks into his new relationship, he called to ask whether I'd have any interest in taking a friend of his new girlfriend to lunch. It seems the friend of the girlfriend had recently ended a relationship, and the girlfriend was trying to find someone new for the friend. I declined, telling my client that I'd recently become involved with someone new, someone from out of town, and that I had no desire to date two women at the same time.

Throughout my four months with Nora, on at least a weekly basis, the client would call to inquire about how "Ohio" was doing, but he would end each call with a reference to his girlfriend's friend, and how she was "still available." At first, he'd merely inquire about my interest ("Are you sure you don't want to take her to lunch?"), but gradually he started to cajole ("Come on, what's the harm in taking her to lunch?"), and eventually to beseech ("Please, do me a favor, I'm begging you, just take her to lunch!"). Obviously, he was trying to be a hero to his new girlfriend by finding some poor schmuck to date the girlfriend's loser of a friend, but I was having none of it. Time and again I'd decline, citing Nora not merely as an excuse, but because, during my time with her, I genuinely had no desire to become involved with anyone else.

But then Nora and I ended things, and before I could get my act together enough to begin my local Internet search, the client called. When I told him, with sadness, that my long-distance relationship had ended, he responded with about six seconds of sympathetic drivel, then said, almost excitedly, "Well now you have no excuse—you have to take this woman to lunch!"

A better man would have turned him down. A better man would have said, "Listen, I just ended a relationship, I'm in no shape to start dating right away, I need some time to get over this, so, please, leave me alone for a while." I didn't, for two reasons. First, he was not merely a client—he was a big client. As long as I was seeing someone else, my refusals had the ring of social correctness to them and he could not allow himself to feel insulted. But now that I was no longer involved with "Ohio," my reluctance to accommodate his efforts to show off for his girlfriend could have had him concluding that perhaps his loyalty as a client was misplaced. I did not want to lose a client over a harmless lunch with a dateless woman. More importantly, I knew from the tenacity of his weekly calls that he was not going to let up on his determination to make this date happen, and so turning him down now would have meant only that I was postponing the inevitable. I was cornered, and I had no choice.

"Okay," I said, "give me her number," thinking to myself, I'll call this loser, I'll take her to lunch, I'll get my client off my back, and then I'll turn my attention to the new romantic frontier: The Internet.

That, at least, was my plan.

* * *

It was Scottish poet Robert Burns who once wrote, "The best laid schemes o' mice an' men / Gang aft a-gley," which, loosely translated, means, "Go ahead, numbskull, make your plan, if you dare." Eager to clear this one hurdle before logging on to the world of Internet dating, I called the loser friend of my client's girlfriend.

Her name was Erin, and our conversation could not have been more lifeless and generic. She was 35, with an 8-year-old daughter and a 4-year-old son. She lived in Boca Raton, and worked in the finance department of a small public company in Fort Lauderdale, not far from my office. She'd been divorced for three years, and (as I knew already) had recently ended another relationship. After 15 or 20 minutes of superficial chit-chat—and not wanting to invest any more time than absolutely necessary before putting this obligatory date behind me—I suggested we meet for lunch later that week, and she accepted.

Three days later, shortly before noon, I sat on a bench in the front reception area of a local restaurant, waiting for Erin to arrive. Mindful that all my prior fix-ups had been disastrous, and not unaware that my client had been unable, for four months, to find anyone else willing to treat this woman to a lunch, I had something less than low expectations—I had no expectations.

Then Erin walked in.

* * *

Whoa.

* * *

There were times—many times—when I'd order something from a catalog, something like a shirt or a watch or a book, and I'd come home each day wondering whether that would be the day when the package would be sitting on my front step. Invariably, the package would fail to appear, until finally, on the day when I'd actually forgotten to think about it, surprise—there it was! The phenomenon's been expressed a hundred different ways—"A watched pot never boils," or "Just when you least expect it," or "When you stop looking for something, that's when you find it"—but the concept is the same. Surprise requires the absence of expectation.

* * *

She looked like a fashion model. Thin—waifish, even—with shoulder length, dirty blonde hair, parted off to the side, and a smile so dazzling it could make you lose your balance. As she stood in the restaurant's open doorway, surveying the waiting area looking for me, she seemed like a picture in a magazine, like an ad for an expensive perfume. I should have stood up, should have walked over and introduced myself, but I couldn't. I was transfixed. I watched in slow motion as she moved forward, gracefully, extending her hand in a gesture of hello, until I realized, with a synaptic jolt, that the gesture was directed to me.

"Hi," she said, "you must be Kenn. I'm Erin."

"Yes," I said, as I stood up to shake her hand. Then, trying my hardest to affect a demeanor of cool confidence in the face of such intimidating beauty, while at the same time wrestling with the split-second decision of whether to say "glad to meet you" or "nice to meet you," I blew it all by blurting out, "Glad to nice you!"

Generously, and in a display of quickness and humor that was as impressive as her good looks, Erin took my hand and said, with a smile, "Well I'm very glad to nice you, too!"

* * *

We niced each other, gladly, for two years after that.

* * *

63

Under different circumstances, I do believe Erin and I could have been happy together permanently. If building a life with her involved only the two of us, I believe we could have made it happen. As a couple, we could have generated enough figurative bricks and mortar to have built a lasting relationship, one that evolved and matured and deepened over time. We were, as a twosome, compatible in almost every way. Perfect? Of course not—perfection in a mate is a fantasy, and an evil one at that, dooming those who pursue it to a life of failure and disappointment. But the indescribable fundamentals that drew me to Erin, and Erin to me, were so deep that our imperfections as a couple actually became integral components of a greater, more fulfilling whole. At no time during our two years together did I ever feel anything less than complete contentment when in her presence, even if we were bickering, and I know she felt the same. We cared about each other. We helped each other. We challenged each other. Probably more important than anything else: We genuinely liked each other.

When two people, never before married and with no children, meet and fall in love in their twenties, they stand like pilgrims on the shore of a fresh new world, hoping to fashion from the untouched wilderness a way of life consistent with their needs and their dreams. When two people, previously married and with two sets of children, meet and fall in love in their thirties or forties, they stand like eager but harried tourists on a busy intersection in a large and foreign city, trying not to lose sight of each other as the crowds and the chaos, the traffic and the noise, tug and shout at each of them from different directions. While the pilgrims' task is daunting, their success, while by no means guaranteed, is limited only by their own capacities, their own desires, and the unpredictability of nature. The tourists' task, on the other hand, is far more difficult, limited not only by capacity, desire, and nature, but by the influence and the demands of others.

For Erin and me, the "others" were our children.

* * *

My situation at the time, while probably not unique, was nevertheless not typical. For most divorced men with children, being a father meant having the kids every other weekend, taking them to dinner on a weeknight once in a while, and attending various significant events. While this description would not have fit me in any event—I was far too involved with my kids, far too connected to them, to have succumbed to such a part-time role—my ex's illness turned the entire paradigm on its head. When I first met Erin, my ex was already nine months into her illness, and she passed away three months later, so from the outset I was pretty much a full-time single parent. This affected our relationship profoundly, as I juggled to accommodate the very real and important needs of my adolescent children, while at the same time trying to indulge my own desire for this new and promising love.

My children's needs were understandably plentiful, from the mundane (carpooling, home-cooking, help with homework, making sure they had the latest clothes, the right school supplies) to the essential (feeling secure, feeling free to grieve, feeling free to mature, feeling unconditionally loved and supported and protected and encouraged). Filling these needs involved more than simply a trip to the mall or adding a computer onto the home network—it involved staying acutely attuned to the day-by-day stages and changes that marked the lives of these two bright teenagers, making sure I was always around, always present, physically and emotionally, ready to offer advice, or solutions, or, perhaps more importantly, just an ear. Good parenting is hard, full-time work, involving an infinite number of aspects and facets, but in my experience the healthiest parent-child relationships always, without exception, have two basic elements: A parent who is always there for the child, and a child who knows the parent is always there.

Having that kind of relationship with my kids, while at the same time working to build and maintain a relationship of the heart with Erin, would have required a delicate balancing act even if no other "children factors" were involved. But other children factors were involved, factors at first obscured by the optimistic glow of new love, but lurking nevertheless, ready to reveal themselves as the glow subsided and the background came more fully into view.

Erin's children were appreciably younger than mine, and were, shall we say, more challenging temperamentally. This didn't matter in the beginning. Nothing mattered in the beginning. In the early stages of my love affair with Erin, every obstacle was surmountable, every red flag laughably insignificant. We were in love, and love conquers all, right?

Well, yes and no. Or, more accurately, no.

* * *

In the second summer of our relationship, as we approached the end of our second year, Erin announced that she wanted to be married. To me. No later than the following summer.

We had talked about marriage before, and in the abstract I was not opposed to the idea, even bringing it up casually on my own every now and again. I loved Erin deeply—I loved the couple we'd become, loved that we were each a fundamental part of the other's life, and loved the thought that this would always be so. After almost two years, my heart still quickened when she entered the room and still melted when she fell asleep in my arms. We had not, however, moved in together—we'd maintained our own households throughout our time as a couple—and so we'd avoided considering, in any real way, the pragmatics of blending our lives and our families more completely. Erin's announcement forced that consideration, and the results, for me, were unsettling.

My children had endured a rather harrowing few years, but life for them was finally starting to stabilize. They did not begrudge my relationship with Erin, although neither did they embrace her as a surrogate parent (nor had that been my desire). To them, Erin was Dad's girlfriend, and she was acceptable in that role. Her children, however, were a different story. To my kids, Erin's daughter and son were tolerable barely, when tolerable at all. This was partly an understandable aversion to sharing me (their only parent) with anyone else's children, and partly it was age-related (teenagers want to spend their time with teenagers, not with children younger than 10). Mostly, though, my kids' negativity toward Erin's daughter and son resulted from fundamental differences in personality types. As any parent can tell you, some kids are easy and some are just plain difficult. Erin's kids, at that time, were difficult. In small doses, my kids could put up with them. In large doses, not so much.

For several weeks after she announced her desire to be married, Erin and I talked. She explained how she yearned to wake up next to someone every morning and to fall asleep next to someone every night, how badly she wanted to share the morning coffee and the morning paper with a loving mate. She described how desperately she wanted her children to have a full-time father figure living under the same roof, and how urgently she wanted to restore for herself and for her kids that conventional, idyllic family environment she'd dreamed of before her own divorce.

I understood it all. I did. And I felt much the same way. I, too, hungered for the blissful luxury of sharing a home and a family with the woman I loved. But I had other realities to consider. Given the several traumatic transitions my kids had weathered in the recent past, could I fairly subject them to another one so soon, particularly one that unquestionably would foment stress and unhappiness? True, I was entitled to my own measure of contentment and fulfillment, but at what price? And could I truly feel happy and fulfilled if my children were resentful, particularly if their resentment rightly stemmed from the belief that I'd chosen my own happiness over theirs? Doesn't parenting—good parenting—require sacrifice?

Erin was not unmindful of my concerns, but she was not persuaded that I had played them out correctly. Yes, she conceded, there were issues with her children, but those issues might just as likely improve under a more stable environment, and yes, my kids might be resentful at first, but that's common in any second marriage and can be lessened and healed as time reveals to them the greater rewards of a full and happy family life.

As I came home one night after yet another of our many such conversations, I eased into my favorite recliner and leaned back, confused and burdened with the weight of what had become not just a difficult decision, but, in a very real sense, an ultimatum. Erin felt we had talked enough. To her, the clock was ticking—it was now early fall, and if we were to be married by next summer, the planning would have to begin soon. My intention, as I sat back in the recliner, was to have a thoughtful, silent conversation with myself, one in which I considered and balanced the two competing categories of variables—those rooted in love, and those rooted in pragmatics—and came to a decision, once and for all. I pushed the recliner all the way back to begin my quiet dialogue, but as I settled in to the padded, leather softness, I noticed something.

It was the silence.

At Erin's house, for the most part, the prevailing environment was noisy and chaotic—the natural by-product of living with two young children—so our discussions during those weeks were tainted and distracted by the stress that reigned as part of the normal order of things. The result was interrupted sentences, lost trains of thought, and always a sense that we'd been unable, by the time I had to leave, to flesh out and express our feelings completely.

Now, here I was, swaddled comfortably within the cushions of my beloved recliner, hoping the silence would help me crystallize my thoughts and arrive at the appropriate decision. Instead, the silence was my answer.

My kids, both in high school at the time, were in their rooms doing homework. Quietly. Call me lucky, call me spoiled—I won't deny either description—but I've been blessed with two great kids, and this was pretty much the usual routine at my house on a school night. Calm. Civilized. Quiet.

I'd always been aware of the contrast between my home environment and Erin's, but until that moment in my recliner I'd never thought of the difference as a choice—I never thought I'd have to choose one lifestyle over the other. In fact, part of what made Erin's more frenzied household endurable to me was the knowledge that my visits there were just that—visits—and that I always had my more peaceful space to come home to. Marrying Erin would change that dramatically, not only for me, but for my kids.

At just the time that Erin wanted us to be married, my son would be going off to college. He'd be wrapped up in both the thrill and the fear of leaving home, of living among strangers and making new friends, of doing his own laundry, making his own meals, fending for himself while acclimating to the burdens of college studies and the pleasures of campus life. Through it all, though, he'd be looking forward, as most collegians do, to that simple joy of coming back during breaks to those familiar comforts of home—*his* home, just as he'd left it. Marrying Erin would change that. Neither my house nor Erin's was large enough to accommodate all of us, so marrying her would require moving. My son would be coming back not to *his* house, but to a new house, to surroundings that were foreign to him, and to a frantic setting that bore no resemblance to the more relaxed environment he'd known as home. Understandably, he'd hate it.

How could I do that to him?

And my daughter. For years she'd been looking forward to the time when her big brother went off to college. She loved him, of course, and would miss him, for sure, but she salivated over the simple luxuries his absence would afford—a bathroom all to herself, the food in the pantry all to herself, our two dogs all to herself. And as much as she looked forward to these perks of his absence, she looked forward even more to one other reward: For the first time in her life, she'd have Daddy all to herself. Marrying Erin would turn all of this upside down. Just at the time when my daughter was anticipating the freedom of an exclusive household and the coziness of an exclusive few years with me, Erin's plan would take all of that away. My beautiful daughter, who'd suffered such bitter grief in just a few short years but who'd come through to a place of stability and contentment, would once again be made miserable.

How could I do that to her?

And what about me? Apart from whether I could ever muster the head or the heart to choose, voluntarily, to move my children from contentment to unhappiness, would I choose to marry Erin even in the absence of my kids' objections? Was the time really right for me? I loved her deeply. But as I listened to the silence that night in my recliner, it spoke to me loudly. Marrying Erin would involve more than merely waking up next to her every morning and coming home to her every night (which, of course, would be wonderful), and it would involve more than the serious and concerted effort necessary to nurture and build a good and lasting life together (which, in its own way, would be wonderful, too). No, marrying Erin would also mean assuming the role of full-time stepparent to two very young and challenging children, at a time when my own children had matured into young-adulthood and were but a few years shy of leaving the nest entirely. It would mean a guarantee of perhaps a decade or more of the harried, often turbulent lifestyle associated with raising two highly active children, and it would mean perhaps a decade or more of living in a world appreciably more stressful than the world I'd created for myself and my own kids.

Marrying Erin would mean giving up the silence.

How could I do that to me?

* * *

As far as I was concerned, it didn't have to end. For two years, my relationship with Erin had been cruising along smoothly, humming like a finely tuned engine. Why couldn't we simply stay on that path? Why couldn't we acknowledge, jointly, our longing for the time when our lives would share the same roof, but also recognize, jointly, that the stars were not yet aligned for that scenario? Our two years together, even though living in separate houses, had been so fulfilling and so enriching, why couldn't we continue to fulfill and enrich each other's lives, in much the same way, until circumstances made living together the more harmonious option for everyone? Finances were not an issue (Erin didn't need my money, and I didn't need hers), nor was raising a family of our own (neither one of us wanted more children), so why was "marriage" such an urgent priority, especially in the face of such obviously bad timing?

Women have since told me that, as a man, I simply don't understand the marriage imperative. Maybe that's true. Maybe my ownership of two testicles prevents me from empathizing with the inherent nesting impulse that has some women yearning, instinctively, for the security of married life. But knowing that more than half the marriages in America end in divorce, and having been married and divorced myself, I've admittedly lost faith in the concept of "the security of married life." To me, married life is no guarantee of security. Married life is married life. Security is security. Sometimes they coincide, sometimes they don't, but one is no promise of the other.

Love, on the other hand, is something else entirely. It doesn't come along very often, and when it does it must be cultivated and nurtured, but it does not require marriage to survive. Erin and I were an unmarried couple, each with our own children and living in separate houses, but we were a couple nevertheless, and I believed we were very much in love. Was marriage forever out of the question? No. But marrying Erin the following summer, in accordance with her desires, would have been a disaster—for my son, for my daughter, for me, and, because of that, for Erin and her kids as well.

Marrying Erin at that time would have doomed our love. Erin didn't see it that way. Erin wanted to be married. My reluctance—even though coupled with a plea that we not give up what we had, and even though not foreclosing the possibility in the future—was, to Erin, a rejection, and it filled her with a resentment that she was simply unable to surmount. And so, notwithstanding our love, our relationship came to an end.

* * *

There's no such thing as a love potion. There's no recipe that assures the flowering of infatuation merely by combining certain predetermined ingredients. Love—and why it happens—is a mystery. When it happens, though, love, itself, becomes a potion. It's a rare and intoxicating mixture of desire and affection, compassion and need, empathy and openness. It's addicting. A tiny taste of love never satisfies, it only increases the appetite for more. Love inspires and motivates. It soothes and heals. It generates comfort and strength, and it can sow the seeds of life itself. It is very, very powerful.

But sometimes, love is not enough.

PART TWO

EDUCATION

CHAPTER SIX—WATER THE PLANTS

Six months passed—six months suffused with varying forms of melancholy. At first, I felt a kind of serene regret—an aching sadness, to be sure, but one buffeted by an almost contented sense of certainty that I'd done the right thing, both for me and for my kids. That morphed during the next couple of months into a more anxious regret, a pining matched with the hope that the phone would ring, that it would be Erin, and she'd be asking if it were too late for her to have a change of heart. Eventually, though, as I neared the sixth month of my post-Erin era, I settled into what can only be described as a resigned regret, a sorrow paired with an acceptance of the fact that, despite all the love and longing, it really, truly, was over. Armed with that acceptance—and with the encouragement of friends and family (including my kids), all of whom convinced me that six months of post-breakup navel-contemplation was more than enough—I resolved to take a chance at finding love again by picking up where I'd left off before Erin smiled her way into my life.

Internet, here I come.

* * *

Finding love again. So many vague concepts—so many familiar-sounding but mysterious and contradictory notions—are hidden within those three seemingly simple words: Finding love again.

Can we really "find" love? Is it the prize at the end of some scavenger hunt, a treasure chest with a blinking light, hidden behind a tree, just waiting for us to figure out the clues to its location? To believe that one can "find" love is to believe that it already exists. But does it? Does a love exist for each of us, just waiting to be found? Or is love more accidental than that? Is love, instead, the random product of luck and happenstance and timing? If so, why bother looking for it? I wasn't expecting to find love with Erin. Erin was a surprise.

And if, as the fairy tales tell us, a love does exist for each of us—if somewhere out there sits "the one"—then are those of us who've loved once already (and who therefore, by definition, have already once located "the one") deluding ourselves by trying to find "the one" (albeit a different "one") yet again? Is there a limit to the number of loves we can experience?

And what are we looking for anyway? When we're out there looking for "love," we're all using the same word, but are we all using the same definition? Yes, love is overpowering and inspiring and exciting, but do we all feel it precisely the same way? The paint store carries hundreds of shades of white. Isn't love like that, too? And with so many shades and variations as we try to find a match, aren't we more likely to get it wrong than to get it right?

Maybe. So what?

* * *

Two and a half years had passed since I'd first considered trying the Internet route to romance. In that time, the options for an online love search had expanded significantly. Where earlier I had located two different services that seemed to be the most widely used, now, in the summer of 2002, I'd found at least half a dozen, each touting its own claim of uniqueness. Some catered to particular religious persuasions, some to socio-economic demographics, while still others tried to sell their size—bigger and therefore more choices, or smaller and therefore more exclusive. Yet regardless of their individual marketing gimmicks, each of the online dating networks worked essentially the same way.

If you wanted to join, you'd first have to provide some objective personal data (age, height, weight, zip code—that sort of thing), check off certain boxes to describe your personality (adventurous, timid, low maintenance, high maintenance), check off other boxes to describe your likes and dislikes (smokers, non-smokers, going out, staying home), and yet other boxes to describe the type of person you were looking for (funny, serious, short, tall). You'd then have to write a series of brief essays in response to certain "topic starters," such as "What are you hoping to find in a mate?" or "About me and what I'm looking for." Finally, you'd have to decide whether to post some pictures of yourself, and whether to pay the monthly fee that would allow you to communicate with other members of the network. (All of the services allowed people to post profiles for free, but without the ability to send and receive e-mails, posting a free profile would do nothing to enhance one's social life.)

Still somewhat tentative about whether I was truly finished licking my wounds over Erin, I decided to start slowly. Picking only one service—the one that seemed to be the most demographically compatible—I provided all the objective data, checked off all the applicable boxes, and set about writing my brief essays.

There were five topics, and all had to be completed. The first one asked me to describe myself.

Hmm, I thought, this is tricky. Most people are not very objective observers of themselves—myself included—and so how likely would I be to provide an accurate description? Sure, I think I'm witty and kind, but is that really who I am, or is that just my own skewed assessment of myself? And what tone should I assume? If I came on too strong, I could sound immodest. If I took a low-key approach, perhaps I'd be overlooked.

The better course, I decided, was not to tackle the question head-on by offering a list of biased, self-conscious adjectives, but to go at the question sideways instead. Here's how I described myself:

> I like New England in the fall . . . good books and old movies . . . spending time with my kids . . . quiet restaurants with good wine, good food, good music, and good company. I like flying to Manhattan for a weekend of theater and museums and walks in Central Park. I like a rainy Sunday every once in a while. I like Paris in the spring (yeah, I know, who doesn't?). I like the feel of the sand under my feet on the beach in Naples, a cool pina colada in my hand at the pool, and a smart, tender, fun-loving woman on the chaise lounge next to me.

Yes, I thought, that's pretty good: Not a laundry list of self-assessment, but instead an invitation for the reader to draw her own conclusions based on what I like and how I express myself.

The next topic asked me to describe the person I'd like to meet. That was easy:

> She has the face and figure of Meg Ryan, and the mind of Madeleine Albright—but don't get those reversed!

Okay, so maybe that was a bit flip (even if entirely accurate). Perhaps I should take another crack at it, one that puts less emphasis on my superficial nature. How about this:

> It's the basics that matter most. If she's smart, funny, tender, and soft . . . if she finds joy in music, in books, in art, in the warmth of her family . . . if she likes fun and laughter, but also quiet moments, holding hands, the couch on a Sunday morning with The New York Times and a fresh pot of coffee . . . if she's brave enough to love . . . then, with perhaps just a touch of magic thrown in for good measure, the rest may quite possibly fall into place.

Yeah, that'll work. Not that I thought it would be easy to find someone fitting such a description, but, hey, if I'm asked to create a wish list, I might as well put it all in there, right?

Next I was asked to describe the perfect first date. This required indulging the fiction that such a thing existed, but, playing along—and eager to get on with the process—I offered up the following:

> Comfortable clothing, nice wine, warm hands, good food, soft lips, and laughter. Not necessarily in that order.

Okay, three essays down, two to go. Looking over my first three responses, I noticed a pattern starting to emerge. It seems I had a definite preference for women who were smart, tender, funny, and soft—and, apparently, I liked good food. While this was hardly a peek into the depths of my soul, nevertheless, for any reader paying attention, it probably did reveal an outward hint or two about me. And wasn't that the point? Perhaps the dating gurus behind this service had a method to their madness. Answered with even a modicum of thought, the essay questions could actually be mildly revealing—and they weren't all that difficult.

Then came the hard one: Describe the ideal relationship.

* * *

Except for the occasional widow, widower, or married person looking for a fling, the members of online dating services—if they're between the ages of 30 and 60—have either never been married, or been married and divorced (at least once). And they're presently unattached.

Think about that for a moment.

Where could one find, in one place, a group of people more empirically clueless about ideal relationships? Yet here we were, each of us, being asked to describe something we'd obviously never experienced.

In fact, though, it was a topic about which I'd given considerable thought. We've all got our wish lists, our rundown of the elements—compatibility, romance, great sex, communication, respect, honesty, great sex—but those inventories are almost beside the point. Obviously, an "ideal" relationship requires something more than a completed checklist of static features. Most relationships start with certain essentials—whatever they may be for any particular couple—but most relationships eventually fail, meaning either that the initial "essentials" were not enough, or that those essentials broke down, or that something else was amiss. Too often, we spend more energy finding a relationship than keeping it—we bask in the achievement (or the luck) of having met someone wonderful, forgetting (or never realizing) that while meeting someone wonderful is a necessary component in the greater objective of a fulfilling and contented connection of hearts, it is only one component. Meeting someone wonderful merely begins a relationship. Sustaining that relationship is something else entirely, and while I do not profess to have yet figured out the entire formula for that, I'm willing to wager that one of the fundamentals is a recognition that the relationship itself—not merely its two participants—must be separately tended and nurtured. Each of my own prior significant relationships— pre-marriage, marriage, even Erin, whose resentment, in the end, inhibited any effort to sustain the relationship—died because one or both of us neglected it. In an ideal relationship, neither party would neglect the whole.

* * *

Having put perhaps too much thought into the topic—I was, after all, filling out a profile on a dating service, not writing a Master's thesis—I distilled my description of the ideal relationship into this:

> One in which both people realize that relationships are dynamic—that they are living, breathing things which grow and change on their own, and, like all living things, must be given constant care and attention to stay alive.

This answer made responding to the final essay both simple and obvious. The final topic asked me to describe what I'd learned from my prior relationships. The answer came to me instantly, in five short words. What had I learned from my prior relationships? This:

Water the plants. Every day.

* * *

That was it. I was done with the questionnaire. All that remained between me and the robust, teeming world of Internet romance was my credit card number and a photo or two of yours truly. Opting for the one-month membership (given the literally hundreds upon hundreds of female members, why would I ever need more than a month to find a mate?), I entered my Visa number, then uploaded two recent photos. Almost instantly, I received an e-mail acknowledging my payment, welcoming me to the online dating community, and advising that my photos would be reviewed and approved in a matter of hours (they screened all photographs to avoid offensive or suggestive postings).

No matter. While I was not about to write to anyone until my pictures were posted, and while I similarly expected no one to write to me without my photos to peruse, I still, as a fully-paid member, was free to navigate throughout the website. As I quickly wound my way through the various different pages and options, I became, to put it mildly, gleeful. This was no AOL "Matchmaker." This was something far more elaborate, and far more seductive.

A "preferences" page allowed me to create an infinite variety of search parameters. If I wanted to see available women between the ages of 35 and 40, I entered those parameters, pushed a button, and there they were: Hundreds of them, page after page, with pictures and descriptions. If I wanted to see available women between 5'0" and 5'4", I entered those parameters, pushed a button, and voila! Dozens of them, followed by dozens more! If I wanted to see only those women who had never before been married, I clicked that box, and up they came, one after the other, an endless stream of single women, each offering herself up to the right man for a lifetime of love and happiness.

I was the proverbial kid, but this was not the proverbial candy store. This was so much sweeter than a candy store. This was a department store! This was a mall! This was The Mall of the Americas! There were blonde stores, brunette stores, redhead stores. There were short women stores and tall women stores, foreign women stores and domestic women stores. There were stores with women who smoked, and stores with women who didn't smoke, stores with women who drank, and stores with women who didn't drink. For a single person shopping for romance, this was—purely and simply—paradise.

Once my pictures were posted, I could introduce myself—from the comfort of my own home, without the slightest inconvenience, and without the potential embarrassment of an in-person rejection—to any female member of this online dating universe. If, after reading my e-mail and checking out my profile, she had any interest in connecting with me, all she had to do was write back, and we'd be on the road to romance. And if she had no interest, that was okay, too—I could simply write to the next one on my list of favorites.

Einstein could not have devised a more perfect system.

After browsing for more than an hour—but hamstrung from sending out any e-mails until my pictures were finally posted—I reluctantly logged off for the night, hopeful that by morning my photos would be placed and I'd be free to introduce myself, via cyberspace, to an assortment of available lovelies.

As I awoke the next morning, I hurried to my computer, logged in to my online smorgasbord of femininitude, and encountered a most pleasant surprise. Not only had my pictures been posted, but during those early morning hours between midnight and dawn, my profile had apparently attracted the attention of a bevy of female insomniacs—at least a dozen unsolicited messages were in my e-mailbox, from women who were fearlessly, boldly, unashamedly making the first approach. This was unbelievable! The world was upside down! Could it possibly be this easy?

Like an eight-year-old at his own birthday party, with a dozen presents stacked up in front of him, I couldn't tear the wrapping off of each gift fast enough. Double-clicking on the first e-mail, I was certain, even before it opened, that I'd have no choice but to fall in love with this woman. How could I not? Merely by writing to me, hadn't she already revealed so many good things about herself—her guts, her initiative, her ability to discern an intelligent profile, her attraction to my looks? Before reading the first word of her e-mail, I'd practically convinced myself—this was a done deal!

Then the e-mail opened and I read her brief note:

> I liked your profile. You are cute. But
> what happened to your plants?

Uh-oh.

CHAPTER SEVEN—BUTT SNIFFING

Okay, so maybe I was foolish to believe it would be that easy. Chalk it up to being swept away by the early, gluttonous euphoria of it all. While initially allowing for the possibility that this first woman was simply a literalist—I mean, not everyone readily grasps a subtle metaphor—a review of her profile left little doubt that, despite our common interest in botany, we would not be well-suited for one another. With a writing style that suggested she'd be better off with someone less concerned than I about the working relationship between words and sentences, her e-mail and her listing taught me an important first lesson in Internet dating: Just because someone's been sold on your profile doesn't mean you necessarily want to make the sale.

"Thank you very much for your e-mail," I wrote in response. "While I'm flattered by your interest, I don't think we'd make a good match. Best wishes, and good luck in your search."

Wasn't this what I was supposed to do? Wasn't it proper to acknowledge a woman's overture, even if to decline? To me, it seemed not only appropriate, but necessary, not merely out of common courtesy, but also because of the extraordinary nature of the situation. My experience in the dating world, though admittedly limited at the time, was that a woman rarely made the first approach, so a woman who was audacious enough to take that first step— even if she were wholly unsuitable for me—deserved, at the very least, an acknowledgment and a response. Didn't she?

She must have been online when I sent my note, as no more than five minutes later—while still browsing through the rest of the inquiries my profile had generated—I received yet another e-mail from pursuer number one:

> How could you say we would not
> match!? You have not even met me!?
> That is so shallow!!!!

What? Was she kidding? Was this total stranger, this anonymous combination of checked boxes and meandering essays—was she, actually, trying to argue with me over a matter of personal taste and preference? Here I was, aiming to be respectful and polite by offering an acknowledgment of her interest coupled with a gentle "no thank you," but rather than accepting the good faith of my gesture, she seemed, instead, to be challenging it. What gives? Is this supposed to make me change my mind? Is this what happens on these dating sites?

Suckered in, I responded:

> Please forgive me if I've hurt your
> feelings—that was not my intention.
> While I'm sure we would not be
> compatible, I felt it would be rude of me
> simply not to respond at all. Please
> accept my response in that spirit. I wish
> you only the best.

Within minutes, her reply: "Please forget I ever wrote to you!!"

* * *

One of the realities of life in the digital age is the shortening of time between various events. Correcting errors in a typed document used to take a couple of hours. Delivering a letter used to take a few days. Catching a television rerun used to require the passing of seasons. Not any more. Now, you can even break up with someone before ever being involved.

*　*　*

Later on in my travels through the world of cyber-dating, I'd come to understand that first woman's anger—an anger not so much directed at me, but borne, instead, from the frustration that a universe barely eight inches away from one's face, and filled with such ever-replenishing plenty, could yield so little. For now, though, the lesson learned from her nasty retort was that even the most polite demurral might not be accepted in the same respectful spirit in which it is offered. Oh, well. That would not stop me, during those first few weeks of my online membership, from continuing to respond to every woman bold enough to write to me, even if my response was to decline—which is how I handled all of those first dozen or so e-mails. But even though none of those initial inquiries appealed to me, still, I was unbowed. While I'd certainly anticipated a sunnier beginning to my online dating experience, my sense of optimism was not affected. After all, I was hardly limited to those initial women—I was now a fully-subscribed, paid-up, online dating service member, and was therefore free to chart my own course, to pursue whomever I wanted, with no limits.

Which is what I did. And after many months of trial, error, deduction, and embarrassment—involving dozens upon dozens of first dates—I'd navigated enough of the online dating terrain to have figured out, pretty much, the lay of the land.

*　*　*

There are four phases to meeting someone on an Internet dating service. With few, if any, exceptions, the phases must occur in order—one through four—and a failure to pass successfully through any phase will, in virtually all cases, prevent the process from continuing.

The first phase—which is the only stage that is non-interactive—is the profile phase. This is the starting point, the point at which you first peruse a profile to determine whether the overall package, as portrayed in the listing, is something you'd like to pursue. In a very real sense, it's no different from browsing through one of those glossy, four-color real estate booklets. If you're in the market for a four bedroom, three bath, Mediterranean style home in Boca Raton, you'll probably spend little if any time reading about the two bedroom villa in Hallandale, although you might consider the four bedroom, two-and-a-half bath home on the Boca/Delray border. Similarly, if you've decided that you're best suited with a petite woman between the ages of 40 and 50 who lives within ten miles of your front door in Coral Springs, you'll certainly look at the profiles of women who fit that description, and you'll probably look at those who are perhaps a little younger, a little older, or a little farther away—but you're not likely to have any interest in the large, 58-year-old woman from South Miami.

However, as anyone who's ever scanned one of those real estate booklets knows, the imperative to sell can result in the use of misleading jargon and descriptions—both verbal and visual—designed to lure the unsuspecting prospect past that first phase of non-interactive browsing. In the real estate booklet, the listing for the house with a poorly maintained exterior will feature a picture of the beautiful view from the backyard. The blurb for the home with the dated kitchen cabinets will refer to the kitchen as "vintage." And the ad for the house in which all of the bedrooms are dreadfully small will refer to the bedrooms as "charming." In the world of real estate sales, careful photo selection and clever use of verbiage are designed to hide or minimize the negative and to enhance or exaggerate the positive.

So, too—only more so—in the world of online romance, where the hunger for love will often not merely blur, but totally erase, the fine line between overstatement and dishonesty.

And so, for instance, I've learned that a 175-pound, 5'4" woman—a woman who might accurately be described as "tending toward large," or perhaps "zaftig"—will list her body type as "medium build," and that when a woman is older than 45, there's a possibility that the age shown in her profile will be merely an approximation.

I've learned that pictures can be deceiving. A single headshot—even if attractive—usually omits the balance of the woman's body for a reason. Professionally prepared glamour shots, when unaccompanied by other, more candid photos, usually do a better job of depicting makeup and clothing than the real-life appearance of the subject. And profiles with only one photo, no matter how great the photo, should be approached with caution—everyone has at least one great picture, but a woman who really looks as great as she's depicted in that photo will usually share a few more.

I've learned that pictures can also be revealing. A woman past 40 who poses in a bikini top is usually flaunting a recent enhancement (or two) to her anatomy. A woman with no children who poses with her dog or her cat is usually telegraphing the message that her pet is like a surrogate child, and must be treated accordingly. And a woman who posts a picture of herself in the arms of another man (yes, they're out there—more than you'd believe) has usually never given a valedictory address.

I've learned that despite the actual content of their essays, women who use only capital letters ("I'M A DOWN TO EARTH GAL WHO'S NOT INTO THEATRICS"), by and large, have personality types that tend toward the theatrical, if not the hysterical, as do women who end sentences with multiple exclamation points or who constantly interrupt their own essays with, "LOL!"

I've learned that some people don't even write their own profiles, leaving the task to friends, relatives, or sometimes to paid consultants, and I've even had one date with a woman who, when questioned about the lack of any similarity between her picture and her in-person appearance, confessed that the photo in her profile was actually a picture of her sister.

At first, I was puzzled by all the chicanery. When a woman who listed her age as 43 showed up for our date looking every bit the 54 she really was, I asked her why she'd lied.

"Oh, come on," she answered, "if I listed my real age, would we be sitting here right now?" I smiled politely, thinking to myself, well, no, but we're not gonna be sitting here 20 minutes from now, either. And we weren't. But her answer clued me in to the ethos of it all.

While a substantial number of misleading profiles are from members employing the sincere but often deluded "just meet me" approach ("I know I'm not being honest, but if he'll just meet me, he'll fall in love with me, and he won't be bothered by the means I used to get him here"), most misleading listings arise from the more mercenary, less romantic realization that one's profile is only one amid hundreds of others (all no further than a finger click away), and that measures must be taken to stand out from among the reams of competition.

This is not to suggest that all online profiles are dishonest or exaggerated (they're not), or that men don't employ the same tactics (they do, and with just as much frequency). But for the same reason that few brokers would succeed by running ads touting used homes with faded exteriors, old cabinets, and small bedrooms, in the world of online dating, members without an appealing profile might just as well turn off their computers, put on their pajamas, and crawl into bed with a good book. Alone. Avoiding such a fate often requires puffery, and so the vast majority of all the exaggeration, overstatement, and outright lying in online profiles is nothing more or less than a tribute to the importance of the profile as the first phase in the progression toward online romance.

* * *

Phase two is the e-mail phase.

You've found a striking prospect. Her pictures are adorable, she's age and size appropriate, she's geographically desirable, and her essays consist of fully formed sentences. You can either take the passive approach—sit back, wait for her to find your listing, then hope she breaks the ice by writing to you—or you can take the initiative with a quick e-mail asking her to check out your profile and to write back if she's got any interest. Easy enough, yes?

No.

There's more to it than that. Much more.

Within the first few weeks of my online membership, I'd figured out that the chances of a woman sending an unsolicited e-mail to me were inversely proportional to her level of attractiveness. This makes sense, of course—the more attractive a woman's profile, the more likely she is to be receiving a high volume of inquiries, which lessens both her need and her incentive for sending out feelers of her own. It also helps explain why none of those first dozen or so e-mails I'd received, nor any of the couple dozen more that followed in the coming weeks, had any appeal to me. The more desirable women would not be coming to me—I'd have to go searching for them.

But for reasons I did not initially understand, my first few attempts at initiating an e-mail dialogue with desirable women resulted in a particularly frustrating type of failure: My e-mail advances were not rejected—they were ignored.

What was I doing wrong? Were my e-mails even getting through? Was I pushing the wrong button? Am I intuitively attracted to rude women? While I hardly expected universally positive responses, any response, even a rejection, would have been preferable to being ignored. Was there some protocol of which I was unaware?

Eventually, I figured it out. My e-mails were victimized by the three "C"s of online dating communication: Custom, Capacity, and Content.

On the custom front, the accepted norm on Internet dating sites—regardless of how anti-social it may seem—is that most people simply don't send "thanks, but no thanks" responses to pursuers in whom they have no interest (which may help explain why that first woman was so insulted by mine). Perhaps the lack of real-time, face-to-face communication makes it easier to ignore someone's approach, or perhaps the avoidance of arguments with spurned suitors—arguments fostered by the ease and anonymity of e-mail—makes ignoring an unwanted approach the wisest course. Whatever the reason, the custom exists:

In most cases, like it or not, unappealing overtures are simply ignored.

On the capacity front, the sheer volume of e-mails received by attractive women renders responding to all of them impossible. While nice-looking men in their 40's, with decent profiles, can receive dozens of inquiries, nice-looking women in their late 30's and early 40's can receive hundreds. They receive inquiries from men in other cities, other states, and other countries. They receive inquiries from men who are twenty years younger, from men who are thirty years older, and from every age group in between (a range of 50 years!). And then there are the inquiries from other women. Talk to any attractive woman after her first week on an Internet dating site, and invariably she'll describe it in one word: Overwhelming. Reading all the e-mails is burdensome enough. Responding to them all is beyond anyone's reasonable capacity.

On the content front, I started out with an erroneous assumption. I assumed that any woman to whom I sent an e-mail would undoubtedly peruse my profile, and would respond (or not) on the basis of that review. Since my profile contained so much useful information, I figured that the content of my e-mail had little purpose other than to direct a prospect to my listing, and so my e-mails during those first few weeks were nothing more than generic invitations to do just that ("Hi, Cindy. Your profile is lovely. Take a look at mine, then let me know if you'd like to chat."). In fact, though, I was wrong. Generic communications make generic first impressions, and coming across as generic—particularly when trying to arouse the interest of a member of the opposite sex—is a turn-off of the first degree. In an e-mail intended to capture the attention of a potential mate, content matters.

Armed with the insight of the three "C"s, it didn't take me long to figure out that while there was little I could do about the "custom" of not responding—in most cases, a woman who had no interest was just not going to respond, period—nevertheless, there were real and tangible ways to deal with the issues of "capacity" and "content." With a few adjustments and accommodations, I should be able to finesse those issues and, in so doing, substantially increase the rate of response to my e-mails.

I noticed, for instance, that most attractive women who joined a dating service were still using the service, on a daily basis, many weeks after they first signed on (on most of these services, a person's profile automatically displays the time at which the member last logged in, so keeping track is easy). I also knew from my own experience that the first few weeks of a person's membership were the busiest—e-mails roll in at a feverish pace, and the new member spends hours upon hours perusing page after page of listings—but that the initial chaos subsides after three or four weeks. By then, most of the existing, available, and interested members have already made their e-mail pitches, and the new member has pretty much examined the profile of every member within his or her desired parameters. From all of this I deduced that any attractive woman who'd been on the service for three weeks or more had probably gotten past the initial bombardment, but had not located from among that torrent of e-mail, nor from her review of all the profiles, any man interesting enough to keep her from continuing her online search (else why would she still be online). This meant that an attractive woman who was still logging in more than three weeks after first signing on, after the flow of inquiries had slowed, would probably be receptive to a well-written, non-generic e-mail from someone whose profile she hadn't yet seen—someone who was new. All I had to do to take advantage of this insight was time my first e-mails appropriately, make sure those first e-mails were both substantive and personal—and figure out a way to be new.

As it turns out, this last part was easy. I simply hid my profile.

Most of the online dating services will allow you to configure your profile so that it won't show up in another member's search unless you've actually written to that member. While this may seem counter-intuitive (if no one can see your profile, who will ever write to you?), in actuality it creates a strategic advantage. Since, as we've already established, there is an inverse correlation between a woman's desirability and her willingness to make the first e-mail approach, hiding one's profile from the general membership doesn't materially affect the volume of unsolicited e-mail from attractive prospects. Attractive prospects, by and large, don't send unsolicited e-mail. Instead, hiding your profile stops the flow of undesirable inquiries (thus, by the way, eliminating any etiquette dilemma over whether to succumb to the custom of not responding), but, better yet, it allows you to remain apart and detached from the competing throng—invisible—until you're ready to reveal your presence. With a hidden profile, no matter how long you've been a member of an online dating service, to the women to whom you send an e-mail—and who, because of that e-mail, can now see your profile for the first time—you possess a very appealing attribute: To them, you are new.

The next part—making my e-mails both substantive and personal—was more of a challenge. If I came across a profile that touched me on a core level—the way, for instance, Nora's did a few years earlier—I'd usually be moved enough to write something meaningful, something specifically tailored for the woman in the profile. But coming across such profiles was rare, and in the absence of those rare profiles I could either write to no one, or write to those women (and they were many) whose profiles were perhaps not unique enough to inspire a tailored e-mail, but were nevertheless appealing. Since I hadn't joined the dating service just to become a mere bystander, I chose the latter course, but this meant that in lieu of a separate, inspired e-mail written specifically for each woman (inspiration just doesn't come that easily), I'd need to devise some type of all-purpose e-mail template that could be used on a mass level but still come across as both substantive and personal.

To generate any appreciable response, such an e-mail had to do three things. It had to reveal something about me, it had to establish a rapport, and it had to explain why I was writing to the recipient. And to assuage my sense of angst about using what was, in essence, a fill-in-the-blank form letter, it had to be scrupulously honest. Since virtually all of the profiles that I found appealing had three common characteristics—essays that were smart and down-to-earth, attractive pictures with captivating smiles, and some element, even if indescribable, of sexiness—eventually, I settled on this as my template:

> Here's the deal, [fill in screen name]. I'm a 45-year-old single dad (my ex passed away several years ago) with two great kids. My son (18) is in college, and my daughter (16) is in high school. I've treasured nothing more these past several years than raising them into the responsible, loving young adults they've become, but I'm nearing the day when

the nest will be empty, and I'm ready (I think) to start sharing parts of my world with someone who's ready to share in return. I have no real idea what I'm looking for (such abstract notions tend to wither in the face of real-world chemistry anyway), but a nice meal and some good conversation might be just fine for starters. I'm writing to you because your profile was down-to-earth and smart, you have a great smile, and the picture of you in the [fill in] was kinda sexy.

Check me out, then write back if you feel, as I do, that we might enjoy getting to know each other.

With a substantive, personal e-mail now ready (okay, quasi-personal), and with my profile hidden, all that remained was the timing. For a month, I wrote to no one, but I kept track of the appealing profiles, and when the month had passed I tested my theory by sending my template to a series of attractive women, all of whom had been on the site for more than three weeks.

My theory turned out to be sound. Four out of five women—eighty percent—responded. And all of those who responded—one hundred percent—responded positively. I had mastered phase two—the e-mail phase. Now it was on to phase three.

* * *

While the second phase is critical—you simply cannot meet a woman who won't respond to your e-mail—done correctly it's also very brief. The sole purpose of phase two is to accomplish, as soon as possible, an exchange of phone numbers, thereby facilitating the commencement of phase three: The call.

Unlike phases one and two, in which the purpose of both the profile and the e-mail is to sell oneself, phase three is less about selling than about weeding out. A woman who has responded positively in phase two by sending out her phone number has pretty much decided, barring any blatant gaffes during the phone call, that she's going to meet the guy to whom she sent the number, and the man who's asked for the number has pretty much decided the same thing about her. In the overwhelming majority of cases, the phone call is a fluffy, superfluous, half-hour conversation that inevitably leads to a first date. When it doesn't, the cause is usually thoughtlessness, cluelessness, or revelation.

For instance, the woman who responds to your e-mail on Monday by suggesting that you call her on her cell phone the next day between the hours of 2 and 4 PM (which happens to be the time when she'll be carpooling her kids to dance and karate) is just not thinking. While there are people who could carry on a cell phone conversation underwater if only the phone companies would invent a waterproof phone, no living being, on this or any other planet, has ever had a relaxed, coherent, enjoyable telephone conversation while in a minivan on a weekday between the hours of 2 and 4 PM. Scheduling that first call without forethought—without making sure that the timing and the conditions will allow for a relatively uninterrupted, undistracted period of about thirty minutes or so—can bring all forward motion to a halt.

Similarly, the woman who, during the first call—cluelessly, and with a droll, deadpan affect—talks about her financial difficulties, her ongoing battles with her ex, her inability to control her violent son, or her doubts about "the whole rehab thing," gets credit and bonus points for honesty—but less than her fair share of dates.

And the woman who reveals for the first time in the phone call that portions of her profile are incomplete, if not inaccurate—that she actually has four children, not two, or that her condo actually belongs to her parents, who, by the way, also happen to be living there—may have difficulty converting every phone call into a face-to-face encounter.

Most often, though, the phone call proceeds without incident, a mostly light-hearted, superficial accounting of one's work, kids, and leisure pursuits. In fact, for a lot of people the most difficult aspect of the phone call is not the uncovering of some disqualifier, but remembering what's been discussed with whom. It is not uncommon for a member to have a first phone call with two, three, even four different people in any given day, and recalling at the end of the day whether you discussed your recent ski trip with Patti or with Caren can be a challenge. I know some members who actually take notes. But in the absence of some glaring disqualifier, and regardless of the means one uses to keep track of what's been said to whom, the fundamental purpose of phase three is to advance the mutual interest that's been sparked in the profile and e-mail phases by setting up an actual meeting. The first phone call is but a short connecting flight—a brief but necessary conveyance—to phase four: The first date.

* * *

You're ready. Her profile was spectacular. Her response to your e-mail was quick and inviting. Your telephone conversation was nothing less than delightful. You're now waiting for her to arrive, more relaxed and confident than on those last few fix-ups because for this first date you've had the benefit of so much more information. Then, finally, you meet. And suddenly you realize that while you would not be sitting there had you not carefully and studiously wound your way through phases one, two, and three, those phases—while certainly useful up to this point—no longer have any relevance going forward. Phase four is all about chemistry.

One might logically expect that an attraction to a profile, a connection via e-mail, and a breezy telephone conversation, particularly when they progress on a seemingly upward arc, would combine more often than not to spark some fireworks on a first date. In fact, though, it just isn't so— one doesn't necessarily follow the other.

Profiles, e-mails, and phone calls are necessary, unavoidable stages in the online search for love. They increase the amount of insight and information one can possess about a yet-to-be-introduced potential lover, and they facilitate access to a far larger pool of prospects than one would ever be able to locate through standard, old-style fix-ups. But, contrary to the assertions of some of the online dating sites, they are neither predictors nor indicators of chemistry. Only when you're sitting across from someone, only when you're close enough to touch each other, only when you're feeling that silent combination of comfort and yearning, that pull, that magic that makes it seem as though everyone else has disappeared, as though you've stumbled onto someone you must have loved in a prior life—only then can you know that there's chemistry between you and a potential lover. That can only happen in person, and it can't be accurately predicted on the basis of profiles, e-mails, or phone calls. Phases one, two, and three will bring you to phase four, but when you arrive at that first date, phases one, two, and three catch a bus back home. You can't know whether there's chemistry until you've had that first date. And since chemistry can be an elusive little bugger, you'll likely have to endure the entire process again and again before finding that little piece of magic.

That, at least, was my experience. Time after time I'd see a great profile, get a positive response to my e-mail, and have a delightful telephone conversation, only to have my expectations dashed due to non-existent in-person sparks. The online dating service was providing me with many, many dates—far more than I ever could have experienced through any of the old-fashioned means, and I was grateful for that— but my initial glee at the sheer volume of choices (and at the promise and potential that those choices represented) was giving way to a weary sense of doubt. Having figured out the basics about profiles and e-mails and phone calls, I was wading my way through a veritable ocean of first dates, but with chemistry hiding it's precious little head, I wasn't seeking out a lot of second ones.

* * *

As I returned home one night from yet another disappointing conclusion to phase four, I took my dog, Fred, out for his last walk of the day. My neighborhood is filled with pets, and during this particular month several homes had changed hands resulting in two or three new dogs on my street. Dejected over my date, I had my head down, so I barely noticed a new neighbor walking his dog until Fred yanked on the leash, eager to check out the new kid on the block. As I chatted briefly with the neighbor, I noticed Fred and the new dog doing that which dogs have forever done on meeting each other for the first time. Carefully, cautiously, they circled each other slowly while taking the measure of one another through the use of a particularly explicit olfactory exercise. And at that moment, it hit me. That's what first dates are. That's all they are. They are the means by which two people carefully, cautiously take the measure of each other to determine whether there's any potential for more intimate relations between them.

First dates are the human equivalent of butt sniffing.

CHAPTER EIGHT—NO PENETRATION

"Don't worry," my friends would say, "you'll find her."

I have a loyal and caring group of friends, people I love and cherish, but almost all of them—men and women—are married, and sometimes I get the sense that their interest in my finding a mate is motivated not only by their genuine concern for my happiness, but also by how much more convenient things would be, socially, if I were part of a couple. When I'm invited out with friends, it's rarely with just one couple—it's usually as part of a larger group of three or four pairs, and I'm usually the one sitting at the head of the table, or at the end of the table across from no one. To my friends, when I "find her" I'll not only be able to enjoy all the comfort and warmth of a deep and soulful love, I'll also put an end to all those pesky, odd-numbered dinner reservations. Getting a table for eight is so much easier than getting a table for seven.

But when people say, "Don't, worry, you'll find her," it suggests a fairy-tale notion of some predetermined "her," some singular, identifiable woman whom destiny has hidden away as part of some cruel "Where's Waldo" test of skill and endurance.

I don't believe in that. I don't believe that some mystical force has jiggered the game by creating for each of us, from among the billions of people on this planet, only one person with whom we can create a relationship of true love and compatibility. I don't even believe it's one in a million. While I'll acknowledge that finding someone with whom you can fall in love, and stay in love, is rare, my instincts tell me it's probably more of a one in two hundred proposition. Of course, that doesn't necessarily require two hundred first dates before meeting a permanent love—she could just as easily be number seven as number 198—it just means that she's somewhere within that pool.

Thanks to the Internet, I'm currently at 22—and counting.

* * *

Sometimes you know it's going nowhere before the first drink has even been poured. Off-putting quirks, traits, or tendencies that get missed during the innocuous first phone call often have a way of presenting themselves within minutes of the initial face-to-face.

With Lucy, a 41-year-old massage therapist, it was when she pulled up to the restaurant in a car that had the word "Massage-Mobile" painted on both sides, as well as a logo with the slogan "Let My Hands Relax You" painted onto the trunk.

Then there was Rena, the 46-year-old executive director of a local non-profit organization. When she arrived at the bar looking very striking in her black slacks, black top, and black scarf, I mentioned how nice she looked in black.

"Thank you," she said, "it's all I wear."

I laughed, impressed with her snappy repartee, but she interrupted me: "No, I'm not kidding. I only wear black."

I gave her one of those arched eyebrow looks, not quite sure whether she was pulling my leg.

"Yes," she continued, "it's just my thing, I suppose. I only wear black. Everything in my closet is black. My jeans are black. My skirts are all black. My tops are black. It's like my trademark. Here, look," she said, as she reached into the neckline of her blouse to show me the black shoulder-strap of her bra.

Bemused, I raised my glass and said, "Well, here's to trademark infringement."

She looked at me like I was an idiot. Note to self: Don't joke with women about their trademarks.

And let me not forget Leslie, a gorgeous, 42-year-old, recently-divorced doctor's wife (that's actually a profession in South Florida, and you get to keep the title—"doctor's wife"—even after you're no longer married). Within five minutes of meeting me for the first time, Leslie shamelessly, shockingly revealed how she had methodically antagonized her husband during their brutal divorce, hoping he'd respond with physical abuse so she could have him arrested, then offer to drop the charges if he would waive the terms of their pre-nup.

Check please!

* * *

That's not to say that none of those initial 22 first dates resulted in a second. A few did. In fact, a couple even resulted in a third and a fourth, which presented me with yet a new realization, and a new dilemma.

The realization was that a good first date can usually provide the fuel for at least two more dates with the same person, but the progression from good first date to successful relationship is precarious, and by no means assured. Frequently, by the end of the third or fourth date, you'll either conclude that there's no sustained upward trajectory, or you'll notice something weird or unacceptable about your dinner-mate after all, something not obviously detectable on the first date. In either case, you'll no longer want to continue.

The dilemma was, how does one, after three or four dates, effectuate a stoppage? The protocol after a poor first date is fairly well established—you just don't call her again (I had trouble with this at first, and so I'd send an e-mail the next day thanking my date but acknowledging a "mutual" lack of chemistry, until even my female friends convinced me that sending such e-mails was worse than simply not calling). But after three or four dates, you're in that zone of ambiguity—you're past the initial encounter, some walls have come down, you've perhaps been to each other's home, gotten physical to some degree, but you're not quite officially in a relationship. When you're in that zone of ambiguity, and you decide things have gone as far as you want them to go, what's the right way to let her know?

I was about to receive some guidance.

* * *

Valerie was a 37-year-old, never-married human resource professional. Her profile had a cheery, bubbly feel to it, and our 45-minute phone conversation was likewise easy and light. We ended that first chat by agreeing to meet for dinner two nights later, 8 PM.

I arrived early, of course, and so at first I wasn't too concerned as the minutes ticked away, but as 8:30 rolled around with no sign of my date, I was beginning to wonder whether Valerie would be my first no-show. Finally, at about 8:45—just after I'd resignedly asked the waiter to total my bar tab—she appeared. Breathless and harried, but looking just as adorable as she did in her photos, she apologized profusely.

"Oh my God, I'm so, so sorry," she said as she rushed to sit down, "I got stuck at the office until 7, then had to go home to shower and change, and I didn't have your cell phone number so I couldn't call you. I'm so sorry I'm late, but I'm so glad you didn't leave."

Thin, freshly showered, and genuinely pleased to find me still waiting for her, Valerie could not have been more charming. Despite the wait, and perhaps partly because of the gracious, grateful way she handled it, I liked her. We joked about her frantic efforts to get there on time and my suspicion that I was being stood up, and by the time we looked at our watches it was already 9:30. I suggested we order dinner, but she declined ("When I eat past nine o'clock it keeps me up all night"), so we agreed to put dinner off until the next date, "assuming," she said, "that you'll even want another date with me after this disaster."

I did want another date with her, and four nights later I picked her up at her apartment, pleased to have moved into second date territory, and delighted to find her just as charming and gracious, just as stylish and trim, as the time before. We went to a seafood restaurant famous for offering to pair any of more than a dozen exotic sauces with more than half-a-dozen kinds of fresh fish, so I was perhaps a bit intrigued when she ordered the mahi-mahi with no sauce at all, but, hey, who am I to judge, right? The conversation flowed, the chemistry simmered, and the night hummed along sweetly, ending at her door with a twenty minute exchange of soft embraces and soulful kisses—the perfect dessert for date two, and the perfect appetizer for date three.

* * *

Although noticing something weird or unacceptable sometimes takes a few dates, it does not necessarily occur by happenstance. While the first date is all about passing the initial, figurative smell test, after that first date two different but connected dynamics begin to emerge. In addition to all the romancing and posing and entertaining that carry over from the first encounter, both people during the next few dates engage in the sometimes conscious, sometimes not-so-conscious processes of seek and reveal.

Whether the result of having been burned a time or two, or just a product of the wisdom that comes with age, the "seek" is an internal process that runs non-stop in the back of the brain, like a virus-checking program on a computer, taking note of any obvious factors that might hint at incompatibility over the long term. At the same time, while most people can briefly mask any personal issues that might hinder long-term compatibility, when the issues are fundamental and severe the efforts at hiding them rarely survive more than a handful of dates, resulting, before too long, in "the reveal."

Sometimes the seek finds nothing, and sometimes the reveal is immaterial. When that happens, the potential for a relationship increases. But when the seek and the reveal collide at any time during that first handful of dates—somewhere in that zone of ambiguity—you know you've reached a stopping point. As I picked Valerie up for our third date, my seek and her reveal were about to have a head-on.

* * *

Walking from my car to the restaurant at the start of the date—dinner and a movie—Valerie asked whether I'd like to go with her to a friend's party the next night.

"Sure," I said, thinking to myself, wow, this is going well—we've barely started date three, and already we've made plans for date four.

Then it happened.

We'd been seated, we'd looked over the menus, and the waiter had just recited the evening's specials, one of which was an almond crusted mahi-mahi with some kind of pan-asian sauce. He turned to Valerie for her order.

"Can I have the mahi-mahi, but without the almond crust, and without the sauce—just plain mahi-mahi?"

I don't know why I noticed, but I did. Two dates. Two mahi-mahis. Two no sauces. This had to mean something, and I was fairly sure it wasn't good.

"Wow," I remarked, "you're really a purist when it comes to your fish."

"Just mahi mahi," she said.

"Oh," I said, "so you don't mind sauces or toppings on other types of fish?"

"No," she answered, "I mean I just eat mahi mahi."

"Well what about when you eat meat or chicken?" I asked. "Do you eat those plain, too?"

"No," she said, sounding a bit embarrassed but maybe also a bit annoyed, "I don't eat meat or chicken. I only eat mahi-mahi."

Mr. Seek, I'd like to introduce you to Ms. Reveal.

Why hadn't I noticed it before? Yes, Valerie was thin, and yes, I like thin. And true, I'd not yet seen her naked, not yet even seen her bare legs (she'd worn nice jeans on all our dates). But looking at her now, looking at her wrists, her waist, her narrow torso—Valerie wasn't just thin. Valerie—cheery, engaging, adorable Valerie—was ill.

* * *

A wave of sympathy washed over me. I was now sure that Valerie's reason for not eating on our first date, which seemed so innocuous at the time ("When I eat past nine o'clock it keeps me up all night"), was instead a manifestation of her illness—that first restaurant simply had no mahi-mahi on its menu. How exhausting it must be for her always to have an excuse at the ready, always trying to find a way to deny the undeniable, to hide that which can't be hidden—and that's the least of it. Eating disorders are pernicious. Expensive to treat, hard to shake, and life-threatening, they tend to take over the very existence of the people afflicted, and despite a myriad of different approaches, the success or failure of any particular type of treatment is always a hit-or-miss proposition. Valerie was in the midst of a hard and painful struggle, and I felt genuinely sorry for her. But sitting right alongside that sympathy, right there in the front row seats of my brain, was the cold realization that Valerie and I could go no further.

When you're older than 40, and you're looking for a new beginning, a new chance at love and romance, do you dare to take such a chance with someone whose pre-existing conditions all but guarantee a relationship filled with inordinate struggle and strife? While no successful relationship is ever devoid of all difficulties, and while the prospect of unforeseen challenges looms in connection with any human interaction, there's a difference (isn't there?) between accepting a risk and accepting a certainty. Should a person ever willingly proceed with a romance plagued at the start by known and debilitating maladies? The answer, I think, is that it depends. It depends on the people, and it depends on the maladies. But for this person (me), and this malady (Valerie's eating disorder), the dilemma was not whether to continue, but how to bring things to an end.

We made it through the dinner and the movie, although I declined her invitation for some post-movie snuggling in her apartment—no point walking any farther down that road. The next morning, as I sat at my kitchen table nursing my coffee with the morning paper, I realized I had two predicaments, one immediate and one just shy of immediate.

The immediate predicament was that I had prematurely agreed to date four—the party at her friend's house—and under no circumstances did I now want to follow through with that date. This was a classic blunder on my part, a rookie mistake of the highest order. With seek-and-reveal operating at peak strength during the first five or six dates, one should never—never, never, never—commit to a future date during the middle of one of those early encounters. In fact, the wisest course until after date six (although easier said in theory than done in practice) is not even to suggest the next date until the present one has ended and you've had a night to sleep on it. Often, I'd drive home from a date, impressed and intrigued, only to wake up the next morning feeling much less impressed and much less intrigued. The morning-after test is a must in the early stages. If you've been awake more than ten minutes on the morning after one of those first few dates and you've not yet thought about the woman from the night before, then there's no point pursuing another meeting.

But on this particular morning, I was struggling with the fallout of having carelessly, stupidly pre-empted the morning-after test by agreeing to the next date before the one in progress had ended. Going on this next date, knowing that I had no intention of pursuing Valerie further, would be wrong, not merely because I'd be going under false pretenses (every successive date in the beginning is an implied statement that things are moving in a positive direction), but also because, by introducing me to her friends at a party, Valerie would be suggesting to them (and I would implicitly be endorsing that suggestion) that we were traveling together on a forward path to somewhere. Participating in such a charade would be dishonest on my part, and would only serve to embarrass Valerie in the coming days, when she learned that I'd elected not to proceed further. Clearly, going with her to the party would be a mistake and a disservice. But how was I going to get out of it?

As I wracked my brain for believable excuses, my daughter appeared, having risen from her Saturday morning, teenaged slumber.

"How was the date?" she asked.

This had become a ritual of ours—she had become a minority stakeholder in my dating escapades, always checking out the profiles beforehand and seeking a debrief afterward. As I filled her in on my dinner-and-a-movie with Valerie, she sat attentively, enjoying the suspense of the narrative and groaning in commiseration over the revelation of the eating disorder. But when I ended by sharing my quandary over how to get out of the upcoming party, she instantly offered a solution: "That's easy," she said, "just call and tell her you had food poisoning and you've been throwing up all night— she'll definitely be able to relate."

* * *

It was a mischievous suggestion, tinged with the playful sarcasm that is a way of life in my household—harmless, of course, because it was uttered in private, yet undeniably cynical and mawkish, if not downright ghoulish.

But it worked.

* * *

Valerie was very sympathetic to my gastric distress, and understood completely why I'd have to miss the party. My immediate dilemma was solved. Less immediate, although nevertheless rapidly approaching, was the trickier issue of severing any future expectations on Valerie's part. Dodging the party was one thing. Undoubtedly, though, Valerie would call to check up on me, to see how I was feeling. While I might be able to milk the after-effects of food poisoning for a day or two, before too long she'd ask about getting together again, and I'd have to confront the uncomfortable task of breaking up with someone to whom I was, technically, never attached. What was the protocol? What were my obligations?

By no stretch of the imagination were Valerie and I a couple. We'd been in each other's presence all of three times, for a combined total of maybe ten hours. By the same token, we were no longer strangers. We'd spent a good portion of those ten hours talking openly, and we'd shared at least the first-level intimacy of soft kisses and warm embraces. Neither here nor there, neither in nor out, we were directly within the zone of ambiguity.

Certainly, I couldn't just disappear, nor could I simply evade her phone calls until she stopped calling—that would be rude and obnoxious. On the other hand, after a mere three dates, having a discussion about not seeing each other again seemed almost presumptuous, if not uncalled for. An e-mail, it seemed to me, was probably the perfect compromise, but were my instincts correct on this, or was I just talking myself into a convenient but cowardly way out?

I needed a female perspective—a grown female's perspective (which disqualified my well-meaning but not-yet-worldly daughter)—and I needed it fast. By my calculation, I had, at best, a day or two before Valerie started calling me, and I wanted to beat her to the punch.

Enter my life-long friend, Lisa Goldstein Ruderman (her real name). Lisa and I had been friends since the first day of first grade, and although we'd lost contact for many years while living in different states, we'd recently been reacquainted when she and her husband moved their family from New York to Coral Springs. Having gone through grade school together—having spent virtually every day of those formative years sitting in the same classroom, learning side-by side how to spell, how to read, how to multiply and divide—Lisa and I spoke the same language, a language which at times seemed like a shorthand of half-finished sentences and intuition. Lisa was clearly a friend for life. And because we always communicated on the same wavelength, she was my go-to girl when I needed a woman's perspective—particularly on social matters.

"Lisa," I said over the phone, as I brought her up to speed on the Valerie situation, "help me! What's the right thing to do? My gut's telling me e-mail, but maybe my gut's just looking for the easy way out? Do I have an obligation to call her? Do I have an obligation to meet with her, face-to-face? Do I have any other obligation?"

"Did you sleep with her?" Lisa asked.

"No," I said, "I didn't sleep with her."

Then, calmly but without a second's hesitation, Lisa enunciated a fundamental precept for terminating a zone of ambiguity relationship, a precept remarkable for its pithiness as well as its poetry, and all the more authoritative coming from a woman:

"Kenny," she said, "If there's no penetration, there's no obligation. An e-mail will do just fine."

CHAPTER NINE—CHEMISTRY

Sometimes lying is not merely expedient. Sometimes lying is necessary. Sometimes it's even compassionate.

I could hardly send Valerie an e-mail that referenced her eating disorder. My aim in sending a note was to bow out of this not-quite-yet-a-relationship gracefully, in a manner that minimized any hurt feelings. A mention of her eating issues would undoubtedly have the opposite effect, particularly given the very short-term nature of our acquaintance. Instead, I had to write something that made it clear we wouldn't be seeing each other again, but my reason had to be plausible, and it had to make Valerie appear blameless. Sometime during our previous ten hours of conversation I'd shared with her a brief summary of my relationship with Erin (by the second or third date, previous relationships are usually a topic of conversation). Now, I realized, my relationship with Erin could provide me with more than just the wisdom of experience and the pleasure of memories. It could provide me with my excuse.

This is what I wrote:

> Dear Valerie:
> Last night I received a phone call from Erin, the woman I'd been involved with for two years a while ago. It had been a long time since we'd spoken, but what emerged from the call was a suggestion on her part that perhaps we'd ended things for the wrong reasons. After a very long conversation, and with much soul-searching, we both agreed, for the

sake of all we'd shared in the past, to
give it another try.

I've very much enjoyed getting to know
you during our few times together. You
are a sweet, smart, delightful woman,
and I wish you only the best as you
pursue what we're all seeking: A love
that nurtures and endures.

Kenny

Yes, the Erin part was a lie. It was a bald-faced,
unequivocal, made-up-out-of-thin-air lie. But it wasn't a
malicious lie. In fact, it was the opposite. It was a benign lie—
a lie told to achieve an undeniably necessary result that, if
achieved through truth, would have come with an
unnecessarily nasty sting. Even if Valerie doubted it—even if,
on reading my note, she concluded that I was a cretinous
jerk, a spineless fool, or both—still, better that than to throw
salt in her wounds with the truth. My e-mail was a lie. But it
was a charitable lie.

In all likelihood, I'd be making more donations in the
future.

* * *

That is not to suggest that every woman I met was
desirous of me. Far from it. As the count of my first dates
climbed into the mid-thirties, the split between those women
with no interest in me and those with any interest at all was
running about even.

Sometimes, as with Geri—a stunning, 41-year-old
homemaker with two teenaged children—the disappointment

was obvious and immediate. One of the few women to arrive at the first date even earlier than I, Geri was already seated at the bar when I walked in.

"Listen," she said very pointedly after I introduced myself, "I want you to know that I've just ended a relationship, and I'm not ready for another one, so this isn't going anywhere, do you understand?"

Since not a hint of this had been revealed in our prior 30-minute telephone conversation, I could only assume from her abrupt greeting that, after seeing me in the flesh, Geri simply wasn't that impressed. Fair enough.

Other times—as with Andrea, a 39-year-old, raven-haired court reporter—the disappointment was less apparent and less instantaneous. Andrea and I seemed to click immediately, swapping stories, sharing laughs, with lots of arm touching, lots of asking the waiter to give us just another couple of minutes to look at our menus. By the time I walked her to her car the electricity between us was surging, so much so that after opening her car door and throwing her purse onto the front seat, she wrapped her arms around me, brought her lips to mine, then thrust her tongue so far down my throat I think she actually bruised my left lung. Nevertheless, I must have failed her morning-after test, since my phone call the next day, as well as the second call the day after, and the third call the day after that, all went unreturned.

And in much the same way that it took me a few dates to realize Valerie and I could go no further, so, too, did some women take a few dates to decide the same thing about me. There was Cheryl, a 40-year-old high school social studies teacher, divorced but with no kids. Our first two dates moved on a nice upward arc, and she seemed pleased and eager when, for our third date, I asked her to join me in seeing Luciano Pavarotti, who was coming to town as part of what seemed like an endless series of farewell tours. But from the moment I picked her up on the night of the concert, Cheryl made it clear, through her actions if not her words, that she'd had a change of heart. Her seek had obviously found something off-putting in my reveal, and the result was that she'd rather have been anywhere but at a Pavarotti concert, and with anyone other than me.

She resisted my effort to take her hand as we walked from the parking lot to the concert hall ("Sorry, I'm just not a hand-holder"), then complained about the venue ("The acoustics suck in here") and wondered aloud during the first half of the show how anyone could possible enjoy this type of music. During intermission she told me that rather than sit through the whole performance, she might have to stretch her legs at some point during the next portion of the show, and four songs into the second half, with her crossing and uncrossing her legs every three seconds in an obviously restless display of boredom, I finally turned to her and said, "Let's go."

"Oh really," she said, "you wouldn't mind leaving?" No, I thought to myself, I'd rather stay here with your legs rotating like an oscillating fan, creating a tornado-like vortex that threatens to lift even Pavarotti himself and hurl him against the Jumbotron like a giant Slurpee. "No, it's okay," I said, "Let's go."

I drove her home in silence and never saw her again.

And then, of course, there was Susan. On the morning after our third date, Susan sent an e-mail telling me that I was warm, kind, and charming—but that after a long phone conversation and much soul-searching, she was getting back together with her old boyfriend.

Touché, Susan.

No, I wasn't wowing every woman I came across. Who does? But even if I sparked an interest in only half of the women I was meeting, still, I was meeting a lot of women—and half of a lot is still a lot. The problem was— whether I saw someone once or half-a-dozen times, whether we slept together or not—nothing seemed to be taking hold. The chemistry necessary for any genuine, long-term adhesion just wasn't happening.

And I wasn't the only one experiencing this phenomenon. Not only was I hearing the same lament from the women I'd been meeting, I was gleaning the same story, albeit indirectly, from the dating service itself. Many—no, most—of the women whose profiles I'd noticed when I first signed on, those many months ago, were still on the service, logging in on a daily basis, signaling by their presence that they, too, were coming up short in the hunt for something long-term.

As I drove home from yet another first date—Bonnie, 43 years old with a 12-year-old daughter—a notion started swirling in my head. Maybe the problem wasn't a lack of chemistry. Maybe the problem was the whole notion of chemistry itself.

Bonnie was petite, attractive, and bright. She owned her own home in a nice neighborhood, had an executive-level position at a regional bank, and, like me, endured the death of her ex-spouse from a terminal illness shortly after their divorce. We had similar interests, similar values, and seemed to be at similar stages in our lives. She even seemed to like me well enough. On paper, the fit looked pretty good. But on that amorphous, nebulous, indefinable "chemistry" scale, Bonnie had generated a big fat zero.

There's no explaining it. Someone can be fine on paper and pleasant in person, but still run a flatline on the old chemistry EKG, and despite all the objective indicia that should have made us a match, I just didn't feel that "zing" on my date with Bonnie.

But as I drove home pondering the entire "chemistry" paradigm, I started wondering: What if the "zing," itself, is a fallacy? What if the "zing" is nothing more than a false promise? The accepted notion is that a deep and lasting love begins with chemistry, but what if that accepted notion is just a lie? My marriage began with chemistry, and where did that lead? Nora and I had chemistry. Erin and I had chemistry. My high school girlfriend, my college girlfriend—every one of my meaningful relationships began with the spark of chemistry, as did several online dating flings that resulted in sex but never made it past six or seven dates. Where are all of those relationships now? As a predictor of enduring love, chemistry had a perfect record with me—a perfect zero.

Ordinarily, my first date with Bonnie, zingless as it was, would have been my last date with Bonnie. But in light of my budding epiphany, perhaps behaving ordinarily— perhaps capriciously crossing her off the list as chemically deficient after only one date—was exactly the wrong thing to do. Perhaps chemistry didn't have to be immediate. Perhaps it could be cultivated. Perhaps, with all the other objective indicators lining up in the plus column, the right thing, instead, was to go out with Bonnie again, and then again, and then again and again, letting the chemical processes simmer, steadily, like a pot of cool water on a hot flame that builds gradually to a steaming boil. By lusting for chemistry on a first date, aren't we all just seeking instantaneous heat? And isn't instantaneous heat just another name for a flash in the pan? How much promise does that hold?

I called Bonnie the next day.

* * *

The more I got to know her, the more impressed I became with her story. Her parents divorced when she was in grade school, and her father pretty much disappeared after that, leaving her and her mother with very little support, financial or emotional. Unable to afford the luxury of college, she took a minimum-wage bank job fresh out of high school, and soon thereafter met and married her now deceased ex-husband. The marriage was relatively grim, its only bright spot being the birth of her daughter, whom she cherished. By the time her daughter was three years old—which was nine years ago—the marriage had ended, leaving Bonnie situated much the way her mother had been a generation earlier.

The past nine years, though, had been good to Bonnie. Through luck, pluck and brains she'd worked her way up from entry-level to executive at the bank, creating not only a comfortable life for her daughter and herself, but also a career of which she was justifiably proud. Her ex's illness and death shortly after their divorce was a tragedy, of course—one to which I could certainly relate—but her daughter was very young at the time, and, judging from Bonnie's description, the intervening years for both of them had been positive and stable emotionally.

After six dates, I'd developed a growing admiration for Bonnie's come-from-behind character. Many of the women I'd dated were quick to bemoan the struggles of their singlehood—in many cases, understandably so—but Bonnie seemed to possess a calm yet determined spirit that simply refused to get stuck in the mud. I'd also grown impressed with the very attuned, loving way in which she spoke about her daughter. Often a woman's profile would declaim, "My children are the light of my life," but by the second date the same woman would be fantasizing aloud about shipping her kids off to live full-time with their father. Bonnie's expressions of attachment and devotion to her daughter never wavered during our first several encounters, and as a fellow single parent I was developing a genuine sense of kinship toward her.

Still, as important as admiration and kinship may be for the development and sustenance of a healthy relationship, admiration and kinship do not automatically coalesce into chemistry. As I prepared for our seventh date, I'd not yet felt even the slightest bit of zing. The pot of water was still as cool as could be.

* * *

It was inexplicable. Maybe pheromones were to blame. Maybe those microscopic, subnasal flame-sparkers were repelling each other. Maybe it was neurotic—maybe chemistry requires the flipping of mental switches on some subconscious level that has nothing to do with a rational analysis of a prospect's attributes. Or maybe it had nothing at all to do with science. Maybe it required some spiritual dimension, some other-worldly connection we humans were meant to experience, but not to understand.

Whatever. Unless and until some unexpected turn-off presented itself—unless I received some unmistakable warning sign, some flapping red flag waving me off—I was sticking with my crock-pot approach to cooking up some chemistry with Bonnie.

* * *

In the nine years since her divorce, Bonnie had been involved in only one long-term relationship—a three-year romance with a fellow named Scott. Since the end of that relationship almost a year ago, she had not slept with another man, and although she and I, during our last few dates, had engaged in a significant amount of groping and probing, we had not yet gotten naked below the waist. She was hoping to change that tonight.

Contrary to popular myth, no custom dictates the occasion on which two newly-dating people in their forties should have sex for the first time. The commonly cited "three date rule" is a fiction, probably better expressed as the "three date average." For me, four or five dates always seemed the more appropriate milestone, although I'll confess to several impetuous first or second date surrenders. With Bonnie, however, particularly given my ambivalence, I had not been pushing the issue. Clearly, though, the time was upon us, and good that it was—perhaps crossing over into sexual intimacy would stir the chemical cauldron.

For this, our seventh date, Bonnie had arranged for her daughter to sleep at a friend's house, and she'd invited me over for, in her words, "wine, candles, dinner, music, and us."

We would not be playing Scrabble.

* * *

Seven candles flickered from different angles in her bedroom—one on each nightstand, two on a dresser across the room, one to the right on a wall-mounted shelf, and one each on two different pedestals in opposing corners. Together, they surrounded the darkened room with a soft, yellow glow.

When sex occurs during the fourth or fifth date, the scene is rarely this well-scripted. During the fourth or fifth date, there's usually a sense between the couple that something "might" happen on that night, but it's always dependent on how the evening goes, where it ends up, and whether or not any outside interference comes into play. When sex does, indeed, occur on that fourth or fifth date, it's not entirely a surprise but neither is it a sure thing—unlike tonight.

We'd finished off a bottle of chardonnay during dinner, so the heightening sexual tension was balanced nicely with a wine-induced sense of slow-motion relaxation. Six or seven pillows and a thick down comforter enhanced the already soft feel of her bed as we lay there, sharing the first delicate kisses of a very young night. Song after song played gently in the background, each refrain supporting another unhurried embrace. Buttons opened slowly as pieces of clothing fell quietly to the floor. More songs. The warmth of her breasts pressed against my chest, the sweet feel of skin on skin, as the soft kisses continued, uninterrupted, but growing hungrier. Our arms drew us closer, now tighter, as our legs pulled our groins together urgently, in a steady, circular, rhythmic grind. More songs. I slid my hand down her back, underneath her lace panty, in a prelude to removing this last bit of clothing, and as my palm caressed the smooth curves of her behind, she moved her kisses up my cheek, toward the lobe of my ear until, in a breathless pant, ever so softly, she whispered, "There's something I should probably tell you."

The sound of a flag—a big, flapping red one—started to fill my head.

She continued, somewhat hesitantly, still whispering.

"Before Scott and I broke up, he, um...."

"He what?" I whispered back.

"Well," she managed to say, her voice now so soft it was barely audible, "he gave me a little gift."

It was one of those gifts that keeps on giving.

* * *

Putting aside the lack of chemistry, Bonnie's character and integrity had impressed me from the very beginning, and her revelation at that moment not only reinforced, it actually boosted, my admiration for her honesty and her compassion. Unfortunately, it also had the practical effect of moving the pot of water, permanently, from the stove to the freezer— ending for good my experiment at cultivating chemistry.

Some women would say Bonnie never should have told me about her genital herpes. I hope never to date those women. Others will say she picked the wrong time to break the news, to which I would respond, name me a better time.

The fact is that Bonnie's herpes—by itself—was not the dealbreaker for me. While certainly not a plus—make no mistake, herpes definitely falls within the negative column on any analysis of a prospect's pros and cons—nevertheless, with vigilance and the appropriate precautions, it can be managed, as millions of couples can attest. No relationship is free of all obstacles. The difference, though, is that a willingness to manage an obstacle as intrusive as herpes typically requires a strong base of feeling, emotion, and desire—a foundation of chemistry—and as much as I tried to find or create it, that base just wasn't there between Bonnie and me. In the end, it wasn't the herpes that ended my time with Bonnie. It was the absence of chemistry.

* * *

We lay there, deflated. The candles still flickered, the songs continued in the background, the pillows and the comforter still soothed with their softness, but, clearly, the moment—our moment—had passed. Someday, no doubt, Bonnie would meet a man for whom the pull of chemistry would be strong enough to surmount any obstacle, but for this man there was no such pull.

"You know," Bonnie tried feebly, as the two of us lay there on our backs, staring up at the ceiling, "you'd be surprised at how many people have herpes. It's the most commonly transmitted STD."

"Really?" I asked. "I thought that honor belonged to HPV."

"What's HPV?" she asked.

"You know, the virus that transmits genital warts."

"Oh," she said, "yeah. My ex-husband gave me that gift."

CHAPTER TEN—SIGNS

Eight weeks later, I was offered the opportunity to have sex with two women—and I turned it down.

Let me explain.

* * *

Six nights after that last date with Bonnie, I was at a Starbucks on yet another first date. It was not going well.

For one thing, Starbucks is a lousy place for a first date (it was my date's choice). At most Starbucks, the indoor seating consists of either some cushy, low, upholstered armchairs, or some bleached wooden seats at a bistro-style table. The outdoor seating, if any, is no better—usually wrought iron chairs at a rounded, wrought iron table. The problem with these seating arrangements is that they create too much space, too much separation, between the two daters. On a first date, particularly one where the initial vibes are positive, physical proximity to one another—the ability to touch, both incidentally and on purpose—is crucial to enhancing the experience, which is why meeting for a drink at the bar of a nice restaurant is far preferable. When two daters are seated next to each other on stools at a bar, knees tend to brush against knees, a hand might touch a thigh for emphasis during a story, a punchline might be whispered into an ear—little things that chip away at the defensive wall we all hide behind on a first date. Sitting across from each other in those cushy Starbucks armchairs (where your faces are at least five or six feet apart), or at a wooden or wrought iron table (a veritable safety belt against spontaneous touching), just doesn't promote the same level of closeness.

The poor atmosphere, though, was only part of the reason why the date was going nowhere, and a small part at that. The bigger reason had nothing to do with atmospherics, nor even with the incompatible woman sitting across from me in that cushy upholstered chair (she had forgotten to mention over the phone that, in addition to her two college-aged children, she had recently adopted a six-month-old girl). Instead, what was bothering me the most that night was an emerging realization of how repetitive, how stale, how dime-a-dozen the whole process was becoming. Not even a week had passed since my leaving Bonnie's bed in disappointment, yet here I was, out on another first date. No reflection. No looking back. Just the robotic forward motion of proceeding to the next encounter. Something seemed wrong with that.

Months had passed since I'd first joined the dating service—10 months, then 12 months, now 18, now 20—and while I was evolving into a reasonably good dater, I was starting to question whether that was necessarily a good thing. I had not joined the dating service just to become a good dater.

New women were logging in at a rate far greater than the number of weeks in a month, so even if ten years elapsed without my finding a mate, I'd never run out of dating possibilities. But after nearly two years of Internet dating—after meeting almost 50 women without encountering a deep and lasting love—the thought of going on like this for a decade was too disheartening even to consider.

Surely, that would not be my fate. Surely, given the volume of opportunities, a compatible love would not evade me for that long. If I were right about it being a one in two hundred proposition, then, at worst, I was almost a quarter of the way there. Still, as I nursed my coffee at the Starbucks that night (annoyed that a woman not capable of remembering her six-month-old daughter was nevertheless allowed to adopt one), I was having a hard time ignoring a slowly creeping sense of burnout.

Was it time for a breather?

* * *

I'd already taken a few mini-breaks from the dating service. Everyone does. You come home from yet another lousy first date—your fourth or fifth in a row—you log on to the service even before you take off your shoes, you look at the same old faces and a few unappealing new ones, and you say, "That's it, I'm done!" In a fit of pique and resolve, you cancel your membership, vowing never to return to this wasteland of love-chasing losers. And you mean it.

In reality, though, you're like the child whose mother withholds dessert until you've eaten those dreaded peas. You sit there, arms folded, lips pursed angrily, unwavering in your refusal to eat those mealy green dots, claiming not to care about that thick, rich bowl of ice cream with all those nuts and the hot fudge sauce and that sweet, juicy maraschino cherry perched right there on top like a bright red nourishing nipple.

You hate the peas. You love the nipple. You eat the peas.

And so it goes with the dating service. You get disgusted. You quit. You spend two or three weeks sipping coffee at the local Barnes and Noble, indulging the defiant delusion that love, in the form of some beautiful, intelligent, creative stranger, will find you sitting there reading travel books about Ireland—but it doesn't happen. So you return to reality and log back on to the dating service, succumbing to the reasonable conclusion that, however unpleasant and tiresome the process may be, your odds of finding a meaningful romance are better on an online dating service than they are in the travel section of your local bookstore.

This, anyway, was the pattern of my several brief sabbaticals from Internet dating, and as I caffeinated myself at the Starbucks that night, feigning interest as my date droned on unconvincingly about the joys of raising an infant while in one's mid- to late-forties, I decided it was time for another break—only this time, instead of whiling away the hours at some bookstore, I'd spend the downtime at home, in my trusty recliner, trying to figure out what the hell I was really doing.

But then it arrived: The sign.

* * *

Why are we such suckers for the notion that a serendipitous event, if matched with the accident of good timing, must be some type of mystical signal? Why are we so ready to attach meaning to coincidence?

"Wow," you muse, after learning that you and the new person on the other end of the line each have tickets to the same upcoming concert, "I guess we were meant to be there together."

Sometimes the coincidence is barely a coincidence, but still we mine it for any trace that something other than pure chance is at play. "Really? You went to Florida State in the mid-seventies? So did I. Too bad we never met back then. Maybe we just weren't supposed to meet until now."

And sometimes, in our zeal to find evidence that a particular encounter is something more than just the next one on the list, we actually invent both the coincidence and the meaning behind it. "No kidding? Your birthday is May 2nd? That's 5/2. My birthday is February 5th? That's 2/5! How weird is that? Must mean something, eh?"

Why do we indulge such mindgames?

Of course, some will say these are not mindgames at all, that, in fact, there is a meaning and a plan to everything, with signals such as these pointing like road signs toward a fated destination.

I say, nonsense. We play these mindgames—we invent these artificially meaningful connections—because we're desperate. Desperate to find love, of course, but desperate also to believe that love, once found, will never be lost. If love is just an accident, then it's out of our control, which means it can leave just as inexplicably as it arrived. But if true, compatible love is part of some grand, mysterious design, then once found it should be there for keeps, never to disappear. And if that is true, then by attuning ourselves to all the signs and symbols, all the hints and clues that dot the landscape along our journey, we should each be able to tap into that design, solve the mystery, and take control of our own love-destiny once and for all, never again having to fear the loneliness of lovelessness.

It's bullshit, of course. Unless the signs indicate otherwise.

* * *

Home from Starbucks, I turned on my computer for the sole purpose of suspending my membership in the dating service. Break time was here. The clarity of my recliner awaited. All that remained was logging in to the dating service for the purpose of checking out, but as my computer went through the stages of its boot-up routine, my e-mail program— which starts up automatically whenever the computer is turned on—preempted things by ringing with a new message just before I could log in. Oddly, it was from a woman who'd written to me once before, almost two years earlier, during the first few weeks of my dating service membership, and to whom I'd sent one of my "thank you, but I don't think we'd be compatible" responses. Her message now—unexpected as it was—was brief and to the point:

> It's been a while, I know, but I still love your profile. My name is Alison, and this is your last chance.

I couldn't help but smile at such a ballsy approach, and so I opened her profile to figure out why I'd been steered away the first time, and there it was: A blurry head-shot, poorly lighted, showing nothing either distinct or appealing. Except that now, almost two years later, that grainy, nondescript head-shot sat alongside a second picture, and this new, second photo was clear, full-length, and most importantly, cute.

Quite cute.

What are the odds of this happening randomly? Let's remember that I'd long ago hidden my profile, which meant that unless I chose to write to a woman she'd have no way of finding my listing. And even though, technically, I had written to Alison by responding to her initial inquiry, that response was almost two years ago. Who keeps e-mail for that long? And what are the chances that, after all this time, she would arbitrarily choose this particular night—the night on which I'd decided to suspend my membership—to reach out to me yet again. Surely the sequence and the timing of tonight's events—the lousy date, the decision to take a break, then the receipt of Alison's out-of-nowhere e-mail just seconds before effectuating that decision—could not be explained as mere coincidence. Greater forces had to be at play. Clearly, I was meant to meet this woman.

* * *

We fall for it every time.

* * *

There is, of course, no official borderline—no "Welcome to Relationship" billboard—that marks a couple's transformation from "just dating" to "relationship," but there are indicators. Have you had intercourse on more than three separate occasions? Have you met each other's children? Have you met each other's parents? Have you attended a family function together? Do you have each other programmed into your cell phones? Have you gone to dinner as a couple with any married friends? Have you spoken with each other at least once a day for more than a week? Have you shared morning coffee after an evening sleepover on at least two occasions? Have you disclosed your daily menu of prescription medications? Do you have your own toothbrush at the other's residence? Have you jointly commemorated the attainment of any faux "anniversary" (such as the one-month anniversary of your first date, or the two-week anniversary of the first time you made love)? Has either one of you burned a CD for the other? Has either one of you purchased any grocery item for the other? Have you started referring to each other by pet names? Has either one of you farted in the presence of the other?

If you've answered yes to any three of the above, then whether you know it or not, you are in a relationship (although farting counts double, so if you answered "yes" to that one you need only one more "yes" to qualify).

* * *

A successful realtor who was the same age as I, Alison was worldly, attractive, funny, and affectionate, and we clicked immediately. That was a sign, wasn't it? Clicking immediately was rare enough, but when added to her unorthodox e-mail and its strange timing, our clicking had to be something more than just rare. There must have been some purpose behind it all.

Our first date—drinks on a Thursday—was followed by dinner two nights later. As that second date was winding down, Alison asked whether I'd be willing to accompany her the following Saturday to the wedding of a family friend, and I accepted. At the wedding—barely ten days after our first date—I had a chance to meet not only Alison's two daughters (two sweet and friendly girls, ages 17 and 15), but also her parents, her two sisters, and at least half-a-dozen of her friends. Sex followed, as it did again three nights later and yet again two nights after that, and on the following Friday we went to dinner—as a couple—with three other couples who were among my closest friends. The next night, I had Alison over to my house for dinner and a movie—and to be introduced to my daughter (my son was already in college).

Things were moving quickly, but it wasn't just the intoxicating rush of chemistry that propelled us forward (although the chemical rush, coming so soon after the lackluster episode with Bonnie, was certainly very powerful). With Alison, it was more than just the chemistry—it was all the perceptibly potent indicators that seemed to tell me this was more than just a chance encounter. At every step along the way, I was bombarded with unmistakable signals— uncanny coincidences, odd curiosities, cool similarities—all enhancing the initial notion that Alison and I had been not just lucky to meet, but supposed to meet. She lived directly across the street from a friend of mine, so I'd been on her block, mere yards away from her front door, dozens of times—how weird was that? Among her friends at the wedding on our third date were several high school classmates of mine, people I hadn't seen in years but about whom I'd recently been thinking—what were the chances of that? During dinner with my friends, she instantly recognized one of the wives from the days when they grew up together as childhood neighbors in Massachusetts—how freaky was that? One after another, a series of unexplainable links seemed to point, irrefutably, to the conclusion that Alison and I might actually be "meant-to-be," and in no time at all we surrendered to that notion and began walking along the path of couplehood.

Here it was, barely two weeks after our first date, and for the first time since my break-up with Erin I'd moved beyond mere dating and beyond mere sex, into what could only be described—under multiple combinations of the recognized standards—as an actual relationship.

* * *

My friends were ecstatic. Alison was great, everyone liked her, but most importantly, I was no longer just "Kenny." I was now "Kenny and Alison." Dinner invitations came rolling in, as did calls to join other couples at the movies on Saturday nights, and exactly one month after our first date I actually received a written invite to a friend's 50th birthday party, addressed not merely to me and the usual "Guest," but to me and Alison. Boosted by all the peculiar and mysterious signals, I had moved virtually overnight from the world of singles dating to the world of couples events.

Ironically, though, when the rapid pace of a new relationship is aided by the perceived assistance and significance of magical signs, one can tend, at least in the beginning, to ignore or deny the existence of other, not-so-positive signs, even though the not-so-positive ones may be less ephemeral and more rational than the seemingly other-worldly ones.

Alison had an issue. A sexual issue.

* * *

One of the phrases a man likes to hear every now and then, when the lights are low and the words come as a whisper from a beautiful woman, is, "Tonight I want this to be all about you." So imagine my delight when, as the clothes came off for that first time with Alison, she whispered those words to me. First time sex is always an odd mixture of excitement and anxiety, but as an antidote to the anxiety, those nine words work pretty well.

In fact, Alison liked that phrase, using it repeatedly during our first few weeks of sexual exploration, each time finding new, enjoyable, and impressively innovative ways to make the experience all about me.

Soon enough, though, any man would want to turn the tables, not just because of some anthropological impulse to assume the role of conqueror, but also out of a genuine desire to be giving and loving, which carries its own powerful sense of thrill and satisfaction. The best, most satisfying lovemaking requires a willingness to give, but also to take, with both lovers respecting the undeniable reality that inducing pleasure can be as satisfying as succumbing to it.

Alison's problem was this: She couldn't succumb.

* * *

I'd never before been with a woman who was incapable of having an orgasm, so at first the thought hadn't entered my mind, but as I began to press Alison about my rapidly growing desire to, shall we say, share the love, she reluctantly let me in on her frustrating little secret. For reasons she was unable to figure out, she had never been able—not during her pre-marital days, not during her 20 years of marriage, and not during any of her post-martial encounters—to achieve a sexual climax. Not even by herself. Not ever.

I was flabbergasted. I'd heard about such women, but I'd never actually been with one (not knowingly at least), and I'd always assumed that such a problem had to stem from either ignorance or poor technique, both of which, to my mind, were fixable. And so, in the spirit of couplehood, with the tireless determination that accompanies any new romance, and with full cooperation from Alison, who seemed genuinely desirous of breaking through the barrier, I committed myself to fixing the problem.

As if.

Like the bloviating numbskull who thinks he knows the inner workings of his car's internal combustion engine merely because it starts up every time he turns the ignition, I assured Alison that I was the man for the job. "It's part physics," I explained, "part mechanics, and part gymnastics. With a little patience and perseverance thrown in to complete the mix, we'll have you humming in no time." I actually believed what I was saying.

I was, of course, an idiot.

Over the course of the next month, we tried everything the laws of physics, mechanics, and gymnastics would allow. Our efforts were back-breaking. Jaw-breaking. Arthritis-inducing. At one point I almost gave myself a frenectomy (look it up). We tried faucets and spigots and shower massages. We used a vibrator so large and powerful it could have doubled as a lawnmower, and I'm certain that through the sum total of our efforts we actually accelerated global warming. But the result of it all?

Zip. Zilch. Nada. No matter how many different ways I twisted the key, the engine just wouldn't turn over.

Finally, Alison had an idea.

* * *

"You've noticed that arousal is not an issue for me, haven't you?" she asked.

Yes, definitely, I'd noticed that. Actually, I'd not merely noticed it, I was flattered by it. It seemed as though all I had to do was raise an eyebrow and she could be turned on. We'd known each other for just about two months, but we'd gotten an early start at sex, and we'd followed up "early" with "often." From the beginning, Alison was voracious—always eager and hungry. It was very heady stuff, but it made my inability to share with her the powerful release of orgasm even more frustrating.

"Well," she said, "I have a special way of becoming aroused."

Hmm. I'd been assuming it was the way I raised my eyebrow. "Tell me," I said. "What's the special way?"

She paused, giving a look that seemed to betray some doubt over whether she should be telling me this, but before I could coax her along, her doubt dissolved and she began.

"Okay," she said, "here it is: All I have to do to get really turned on...is to think about having sex with a woman."

The silence was awkward but brief—maybe four or five seconds—and I recovered quickly by joking, "No fair—that's my trick!"

"No," she insisted, "I'm serious. For my whole life, all I had to do was think about that, and it always turned me on."

"Okay," I said, calmly, trying hard not to acknowledge the neon quality of this particular sign, "there's nothing wrong with that. Erotic fantasies are a normal part of a healthy sex life. So how do you think that plays into the whole climax scenario?"

She paused again, this time with a nervous smile and a somewhat mischievous look to her eyes.

"Well," she said, "um...maybe...I don't know...maybe if it were you and me...and, like, another woman? Like, maybe that would work? You know?"

* * *

I won't deny the fantasy. Like probably every heterosexual male on the face of the planet, I'd often imagined the sweet pleasure of finding myself sandwiched between two willing, lustful, ridiculously naked women. (Or underneath them. Or juxtaposed in such a way as to resemble a life-sized version of a lanyard. Box-stitch.) The problem with living that fantasy now, with Alison, was two-fold. First, I liked her. And because I liked her, as trite as this may sound—and all my abstract fantasies notwithstanding—I just didn't want to share her. Not this soon, anyway. Sometimes you meet a woman and you know, from the start, that it's just a fling, that for however long it lasts it'll be all about sex and fun, but nothing more. Throw another willing, lustful, ridiculously naked woman into that scenario, and I'd accept the ride without a second thought. I'd cut to the front of the line. But when you've been looking long and hard for something serious, and you find yourself in the second month of what you think might be something real, your head, heart, and every imagined thrill are focused exclusively on being only with that one person who seems to embody the "something real." And, of course, you expect that other person to feel the same way. To suggest a threesome, at just that point in a budding relationship, is more deflating than exciting.

The second problem, though, was an even bigger one, and more obvious. While I had no credentials enabling me to make any professional conclusions, the data laid out before me—Alison's life-long inability to achieve orgasm, her life-long fantasies about being with women, and her attempt, so inappropriately early in a promising relationship, to bring me into her efforts at turning those fantasies into reality—suggested, at the very least, that Alison wrestled with some fairly deep-seated sexual issues. And if I'd learned anything at all during my journey through relations of the heart, it was that deep-seated sexual issues are the equivalent of poison to any long-term relationship.

* * *

There is an important distinction between walking along the path *of* couplehood, and walking along the path *to* couplehood. The former implies a done deal. The latter suggests a maybe. Coaxed and prodded by all the signs and signals, I convinced myself that Alison and I were doing the former. In reality, we were doing the latter. Signs, schmigns. One of the hallucinatory effects of infatuation—apart from seeing signs that don't, in any rational sense, exist—is the sensation of connectedness, the feeling that you've known this person forever, when in fact you barely know the person at all. It's a leap of faith, and while it gets you artificially (and often prematurely) to that point of trust so necessary for those first meaningful exchanges of intimacy, like any leap of faith it requires a certain disconnect from reason. It's nature's little trick, and as a means by which to start a relationship's battery, it works. But whether that battery keeps revving as the initial intoxication subsides depends less on mystical indicators and more on the objective data gleaned from the process of actually getting to know someone.

*　*　*

I told Alison I'd think about it, but the spell was broken. It was over. We were done.

CHAPTER ELEVEN—THE TWO-MONTH SURPRISE

My friend, Robbie Morton, looked like someone had just clunked him in the head with a brick.

We were having dinner—Robbie, his wife Marsha, and I—at a restaurant in New York City. I was in town for a conference, and Robbie and Marsha, who are from Arizona, were in the city to celebrate their 17th wedding anniversary. The Mortons were a great couple—very close, very open, with big hearts, easily tapped senses of humor, and a genuine interest in the well-being of their friends. I'd ended things with Alison barely three weeks earlier, and I'd just finished explaining the reasons why.

Robbie's jaw hung open, his eyes staring at me as though hypnotized, his expression a frozen mixture of shock, sadness, and disbelief.

"What's the matter?" I asked him.

Marsha tried to squelch a giggle, but Robbie said nothing.

"Come on," I said, "out with it. What's with the look?"

Finally, with a shake of his head that seemed to say, "You pathetic little putz," he responded.

"For the past six months," he said, "ever since Marsha and I started planning this anniversary trip, I've been telling her that all I wanted as an anniversary gift was to have sex with her and another woman. And for the past six months, all she's been doing is laughing and telling me, 'Not in this or any other lifetime.' Then you come here and torture me with a story about how a woman not only *offered* you sex with two women, but actually *wanted* it! And to make matters worse, *you turned her down?* So not only can't *I* do it, I can't even enjoy it vicariously through you! I'm...I'm...I don't know what to say! I'm beside myself. I want to cry!"

Marsha's giggle was now a full-throated laugh.

"Look," I explained, "I can certainly understand how any guy, after 17 years of marriage, would be intrigued by the potential thrill of bringing another woman into the bedroom for a night of living out the classic fantasy. I was married for 17 years. Really, I can understand. But would you have wanted another woman in bed with you and Marsha after only your first month together?"

"First *month*?" he barked. "I'd have done it on the first date!"

Robbie's answer dodged the question. The dynamics on a first date are vastly different than after the first month or two.

On a first date, neither person has invested any emotional capital into the mix, and so an offer to live out a fantasy at that early stage can be accepted without any concern about its impact on the emotional component of a nascent relationship. My guess is that had Marsha suggested a threesome on their first date almost two decades ago, Robbie would have accepted gladly, and would have followed that up by seeing Marsha perhaps three of four more times before deciding that, notwithstanding her adventurous, fun-loving nature, she was not the type of woman with whom he'd want to embark on a deep, emotional journey.

By the same token, while I know it's rare, I have heard the occasional stories about people in long-term, faithful, committed relationships who, after many happy and monogamous years together, agree to add a jolt of electricity to their sex lives by bringing a third person into the bedroom for a night of newness and fantasy. But the key to the success of such unconventional experimentation—so I'm told—is a couple's preexisting, solid bond of trust and devotion, a bond nurtured and welded by years of undoubted love and caring.

"Robbie," I said, "you didn't answer my question. Of course you'd have done it on the first night. Any guy would. And of course, if Marsha would oblige, you'd want to do it now—the two of you have been in a safe, secure, loving relationship for years and years, and you just want to share a new thrill with your wife. But take yourself back to that time, a month or two after you first started seeing each other, when you found yourself thinking, 'Hey, I really like this woman, there might actually be something here worth nurturing'— would you really, at that point, have wanted Marsha to bring another woman into the bedroom?"

Robbie looked at Marsha, then at me, then at Marsha again, until finally, with a sigh, he relented, "No, I guess not." Then, almost defiantly, he added "But if she'd offered on that first date, definitely!"

Marsha smiled lovingly at Robbie, took his hand, and said, "Well, Honey, who knows? Maybe on our 20th anniversary."

Robbie owes me. Big time.

* * *

The most ironic coincidence of my relationship with Alison was this: Although unacceptably abbreviated if considered in the context of a serious romance, my time with her was nevertheless a rousing success as a much-needed intermission from Internet dating—which was precisely what I'd been seeking before her unexpected e-mail first arrived.

For those two months with Alison, and for another few weeks thereafter, I'd been free of the hamster-wheel tedium of profiles and e-mails, first calls and first dates. And while certainly, during that time, I'd been caught up in the excitement of the relationship and all the potential it represented, I nevertheless did allow myself, in the midst of it all, to reflect a bit on the process of Internet dating, and on whether computer dating sites were a help or a hindrance in the search for love and romance.

Internet dating, I decided, was a paradox built upon a paradox. It was, at once, both a great thing and a terrible thing, and what made it so great was also precisely what made it so terrible—namely, choice.

Before the advent of cyber-dating, single people past the age of 40 had relatively few options for a chance at romance. Fix-ups, singles functions, bars, the workplace, affairs—those were pretty much the available venues, and the number of prospects afforded by each of those alternatives was relatively small. My guess is that, given the paucity of social opportunities, middle-aged singles were more inclined back then to settle into a relationship with someone who was less than ideal, on the rationale that settling for fifty percent was better than having nothing at all. When you're not sure when (or even whether) the next meal will arrive, you're understandably less choosy about eating whatever's in front of you.

Cyber-dating changed all that. With their ever-replenishing inventory of romantic possibilities, and their concomitant insinuation that the person you've always been looking for is just a click or two away, computer dating sites effectively neuter any imperative to compromise. Your date may possess three-quarters of the traits you think you'd like in a mate, but why settle for three-quarters when a virtually limitless supply of other prospects awaits? Certainly, with so many people still available, you can do better than three-quarters, no?

Well, maybe. But with so many choices, what will be good enough? Four-fifths? Nine-tenths? A hundred percent? A hundred percent plus one? There's something to be said for the freedom of knowing you don't have to settle for less than what you want, but there's something paralyzing about it, too. With their abundance of choices, computer dating sites foment both—the freedom and the paralysis.

* * *

Recognizing the Internet dating paradox was one thing. Mastering that paradox—taking advantage of the freedom without succumbing to the paralysis, with the aim of achieving a real and enduring love—was something else. Several weeks after ending things with Alison—and with a more graduated sense of understanding about the flaws in the process—I logged back on to the dating site, determined this time to balance choice with patience, and to try to be more concerned with overall compatibility and potential than with some mathematical calculation of fractions and percentages.

And, in fact, over the next nine or ten months, my more nuanced approach did seem to yield some dividends, inching me farther along on the relationship path (at least when it came to Internet dating) than at any other period before Alison. For three separate blocks of time during those nine or ten months, with three different women, I'd been able to move past the one-dimensional strictures of casual dating and into the more multi-dimensional realm of early-stage relationships. In each instance, the chemistry, interest, and physical attraction progressed past the first handful of dates—past the initial morning-after tests and the zones of ambiguity—into something that seemed to have emotional potential. In each of these episodes, I genuinely liked the woman, she genuinely seemed to like me, and I found myself indulging the pleasant thought that perhaps I might have found someone with long-term possibilities. But despite all the hope and promise, at a particular moment on my journey with each of these three women, a decisive revelation found me looking for the nearest off-ramp. Not until it happened the third time, though, did I realize I was confronting something definable and not at all uncommon: The two-month surprise.

The two-month surprise is an adjunct to the seek and reveal—it's a part of the means by which we learn important information about a person with whom we're considering couplehood—but with a fundamental difference. In the seek and reveal, the recipient of the information is attuned to receiving it, while the provider is often unaware of supplying the data. In the two-month surprise, the tables are turned. The two-month surprise occurs just after the point at which one's "seek" scope has given the all clear—usually sometime between eight and ten weeks. It's the time at which the two daters have found their first comfort zone with each other and have softened their initial defenses. With the "seek" scope no longer probing for unwitting reveals, and the comfort zone stimulating an environment of familiarity and trust, the stage is set for the purposeful and voluntary revelation by one party of something theretofore held back, and which the other party has not anticipated.

The two-month surprise.

With Sari (47, newly divorced after 25 years of marriage, with two grown sons), it happened in bed, roughly eight weeks after our first date. We were alone, naked, and under the sheets for only the third time. On the two previous occasions, after slow but steadily escalating sessions of kissing, caressing, groping and panting, Sari had stopped us just short of penetration with a somewhat diffident, "I'm not ready for that yet." Of course, on those first two occasions, I respected her hesitation without question, and I even thought I understood it—she'd been faithful to her husband throughout their long marriage, and I was the first man with whom she'd been even slightly intimate since her divorce, so she was no doubt wrestling with issues of trust, anxiety, and insecurity. But when, on this third occasion, she once again interrupted the crescendo just as it was approaching its peak, I thought it only fair, after a respectful, breath-catching pause, to initiate a conversation about her thoughts and expectations on the subject of more definitive physical contact.

"I'm sorry, Kenny," she said, in a tone that was sympathetic yet firm, "but my ex-husband was the only man I've ever slept with, and I don't intend to start a pattern of sleeping around now. Before I sleep with you or anyone else, I'd need to know that it was a permanent thing."

Her choice of words was disquieting.

"Do you mean an 'exclusive' thing," I asked, "because I'd have no problem with that."

"No," she said, "I mean a 'permanent' thing."

Yipes.

The jokester in me wanted to say, "Excuse me, Mrs. Cleaver, let me go get Ward," but Sari was serious. And because she was so serious—because the act of sexual intercourse, for her, even at the age of 47, carried with it a level of significance to which I, as a man more than three decades out of high school, could not subscribe—I was obliged to honor her preference by not merely respecting her wishes, but by severing our relationship before putting any more emotional capital at risk, for either of us.

A few weeks later I met Stephanie. Six months older than I, Stephanie was divorced, had no children, and ran her own small but successful public relations agency. She was well-traveled, had sophisticated tastes, and was wonderfully uninhibited sexually—all of which appealed to me—and apparently she found me appealing as well. By the fourth or fifth week we were seeing each other exclusively, and everything seemed to be proceeding smoothly enough until one night, during our ninth week, when the confluence of a good Pinot Noir, a comfortable couch, and a relaxed atmosphere yielded Stephanie's two-month surprise.

After clinking our glasses and toasting to "us," I off-handedly alluded to recent press reports about how a glass or two of red wine could have a positive impact on one's overall health and well-being. This prompted a more general conversation on the topic of health, which, in turn, led Stephanie to reveal that, from her perspective, each and every healthy day was a gift.

As a notion, Stephanie's comment was both inarguable and innocuous, but something about the way she expressed herself left me feeling as though her sentiment might have had more than just a passing personal component, so I asked: "Do you say that for any reason in particular?"

"Well," she said, "I guess we're far enough along for me to tell you this." She then went on to reveal that both her mother and her mother's mother had passed away from the same type of aggressive cancer, each in her early fifties, and so a few years ago Stephanie underwent genetic testing to determine whether she carried the gene for the same type of malignancy. The results were positive. While she was currently cancer-free, and while she frequently submitted to early-detection screening, nevertheless, she faced a substantial likelihood of contracting and succumbing to the same aggressive cancer that killed her mother and her grandmother, at ages not much older than Stephanie's.

Oh, no.

The noble response would have been to say, "So what? The world could end tomorrow. Life has no guarantees for any of us. Let's just keep walking down the road and see where it might lead." We see it in the movies all the time. But in the movies, such nobility is typically the byproduct of love, ill-fated though it may be. I was not yet in love with Stephanie. Nor was I living in a movie. And while yes, of course, life is unpredictable—no one can know for sure whether a lover who today bears all the markers of fine health might not tomorrow fall victim to some horrible malady—still, there's a difference between what's possible and what's probable. Although divorced at the time of my ex's battle with cancer, I nevertheless endured the trauma, and had to witness and manage, first-hand, the toll it took on my children and our extended family. Having lived through that scenario once already, I had no alternative, in the choice between possible and probable, but to play the odds by walking away from probable.

Then there was Jeannie. Seven years younger than I, never married, with no children, Jeannie's outward manner was somewhat shy and reserved, but she had an infectious, feel-good smile that reflexively caused people to smile and feel good in return. We smiled a lot during those first few weeks of getting to know each other—weeks filled with a steadily and naturally progressing mix of emotional intimacy, physical intimacy, and comfort—but since she lived with what she described as a very territorial cat, she'd been fearful about inviting me in to her apartment, with the result that all of our time together during those first several weeks was spent either out on a date, out at some function, or at my house. On each occasion, if she didn't come to meet me at my place, she'd be waiting outside her front door for me to pick her up.

That changed one evening, at about the nine-week mark. I was on my way over to pick her up for an evening out with friends when she called to say that she was running terribly behind, just then getting into the shower. I was less than five minutes away, so she said she'd take Rascal (her cat) into the bathroom with her, would leave the front door unlocked, and that I should let myself in and relax while she finished showering and getting herself ready.

"I should probably warn you, though," she said, "the place is a bit of a mess."

Five minutes later, with the door unlocked, I entered Jeannie's apartment for the very first time, and there it was: Jeannie's two-month surprise.

Her apartment was not a "bit of a mess." A "bit of a mess," to me, would have been perhaps a day or two of miscellaneous clutter lying around, with maybe some dishes in the sink. Jeannie's place, instead, was a bit of a war zone.

Worn, crumpled clothing was strewn everywhere. Three used and unwashed pans sat on the stove, caked with the remnants of some type of food product, and the door to the microwave oven was gone. A badly soiled litter box stunk up the room, and next to it some evidence that perhaps Rascal hadn't quite mastered the art of rectal aiming. Two dead plants sat on a windowsill, with dried brown leaves on the carpet underneath. Both sides of a double kitchen sink overflowed with dirty glasses, dirty dishes, and dirty flatware. A bag of cat food had been knocked over, with dried food pellets scattered all over the kitchen floor. Everywhere I looked, something screamed filth: A used spatula here, a toilet plunger there, and over in the corner, by the TV, a pile of empty plastic grocery bags and months worth of stacked-up newspapers. The extent of the disarray was beyond anything

I'd seen in my few but plentiful years of dating. The place was, in a word, disgusting.

I heard the bathroom door open down the hall, and in an instant Rascal was at my feet. From Jeannie's description, I was expecting a hissing, clawing, annoying brute, but it turned out that Rascal was anything but. After brushing against my leg sweetly, he purred, rubbed at his own face, then ran off peaceably to sit on a barstool—hardly the territorial menace Jeannie'd been describing all those weeks.

"So," she said, as she appeared from the down the hall, wrapped in a towel, "welcome to the way I live."

"I don't get it," I said, responding to the most immediate of the many incongruities before me, "Rascal's not a terror."

"No," she said, "he's really very sweet, but until I felt like you and I were really solid, I had to come up with some reason for not letting you see my place. Most guys get freaked out when they see what a slob I am, so I wanted to wait until we got to a point where I didn't think it would matter to you."

She had badly miscalculated.

* * *

A few weeks later, I was flipping through the channels on my new satellite TV system. Ironically, installing a satellite system is a sure-fire way of cutting down on one's TV-watching—with several hundred channels, by the time you've scrolled through all of them, anything you might have tagged to watch at the start of your browsing has long since ended, so you end up shutting off the TV without ever actually watching anything from start to finish.

Too many choices. Sound familiar?

Anyway, among the hundreds of different stations on my satellite is an assortment of Lifetime Network channels, all of which are targeted at women and are therefore usually a rapid part of my scroll. But on this particular occasion, as I was flipping my way through the entire panoply, I managed to catch a little fifteen-second snippet from one of those Lifetime Network movies. Two forty-something women were commiserating, with one saying to the other, "You know how you get to a point in a relationship where you either want to see the guy a lot more or a lot less?" After the second woman nods in agreement, the first woman says something like, "Well lately, for me, they've all been landing on the 'lot less' side of that equation."

Wow, I thought—it's not just me. And obviously it's not just a guy thing, either, although for me, that "point" in a relationship—the point where you want to see someone either a lot more or a lot less—was clearly coinciding with the two-month surprise. In fact, looking back through the lens of my Sari/Stephanie/Jeannie trinoculars, I could see that my time with Bonnie and with Alison also ended after revelations occurring at roughly the two-month mark. In my journey through the world of Internet dating, the two-month surprise, for me, had become the equivalent of a dead end.

* * *

But were they really dead ends? Were Bonnie, Alison, Sari, Stephanie, and Jeannie—and, for that matter, I—were we all truly victims of insurmountable issues that revealed themselves at or near the two-month mark in our respective relationships? Or were we, instead, the victims of Internet dating? Were we the victims of too much choice?

If the process were harder—if achieving a date involved more than a simple hunt-and-peck through countless computer profiles, so that dating someone new was an event that might occur, if one were lucky, maybe every couple of months, rather than every couple of nights—would I have been so quick to walk away after only two months, surprise or no surprise? If the possibilities for romance were less immediate and less abundant, might I have been tempted to maintain and prolong any of those relationships by using a more ancient technique, namely, working at it?

On the other hand, isn't that the beauty of Internet dating—that as a result of so much choice, we no longer have to settle for a relationship that requires work, no longer have to fool ourselves into believing that by squeezing a square peg into a round hole we've actually achieved a genuine fit? Assuming the correctness of my "love is a one-in-two-hundred" proposition, finding that "one" in an earlier time had to be a function of luck more than anything else—no realistic means existed in the past by which to arrange two hundred different dates. But with Internet dating services, dating two hundred different people is no longer impossible, and so why settle for a three-quarters relationship when the total package might arrive in your in-box today, or tomorrow, or next month?

The correct answer—if one existed—continued to elude me. I was, however, certain of this: Another burnout point was rapidly approaching.

* * *

Against this backdrop of exhausted, conflicted intellectualizing, I met Laurie. Her profile was unremarkable, with short, generic essays that revealed almost nothing, but I was tired and cranky, so I didn't really care. She was my age, she had a nice face and figure, and she lived close by. In my weary condition, that was enough.

Laurie, as it turned out, was just as drained as I. Overwhelmed and numb from our various failed Internet relationships, neither one of us was in any frame of mind to commence a serious love affair. Each of us needed a break, and in truth, neither of us should have been out on a date with anyone, let alone with the other. But as we shared a couple of hours over drinks that first night, we also shared an undeniably warm feeling of friendly chemistry, leading us to hit upon what seemed to be the ideal stopgap compromise to our mutually miserable states of disillusionment and fatigue. After agreeing that our common weariness rendered each of us, at that point, a poor match for anyone, we determined there would be no harm, while each of us was in such a state of romantic limbo, in seeing each other one night a week—no expectations, no promises, no commitments, just two people with good chemistry sharing one night a week at the movies, or at dinner, or whatever. And at that moment, Laurie bestowed upon me a nickname: I would be her Mr. Friday Night.

It was, for a time, the perfect situation. Clearly, we were not an ideal match—she was a smoker, I was not; my kids were preppy, her kids were goth; my politics were blue state, her politics were red state; I was a meat-eater, she was a vegetarian—but that was all beside the point. In the fog of our fatigue, we each provided the other with a once-a-week beacon of warmth and tenderness—with some pretty good lovemaking thrown in as a bonus.

We both knew the arrangement could not last forever, but my assumption was that it would end when one of us was ready to get back in the hunt for a real and meaningful love affair, one with all the bells and whistles of an honest-to-goodness relationship. I was, therefore, surprised when it ended the way it did.

I had picked Laurie up for our Friday night out—her kids were sleeping at friends' houses, so the plan this time was for sushi at a Japanese restaurant, then to Blockbuster for a movie which we'd watch under the sheets at her townhouse— but as she got into my car she turned to me, almost giddy with excitement, and said, "I've come to a decision, and it's a surprise, and I just can't wait to tell you."

"What's the surprise?" I asked.

"Well," she said, "you've been promoted."

"Promoted?" I asked. "How so?"

"I've been thinking about this for a while," she said, "and I've finally made the decision. You are no longer just Mr. Friday Night. You are now Mr. Friday Night, Mr. Saturday Night, and Mr. One Night During The Week!"

* * *

Well, she was right—I was surprised. Unfortunately, it wasn't a pleasant surprise. I liked Laurie, I liked her a lot, but to me our arrangement was still what we said it would be from the start—and it could never be anything more. As once-a-week comforters, we were wonderful together, but the ingredients for a more meaningful brew simply weren't there, not for me at least. I had not asked to be "promoted"— flattering though it was—and while I was probably naïve not at least to have anticipated that one of us might get sucked in, that didn't alter the reality that Laurie and I were no longer reading from the same page.

Yes, I was surprised, although I should have seen it coming. The timing was impeccable. I'd been seeing her for two months.

CHAPTER TWELVE—NEVADA

If Benjamin Franklin was right—if the definition of insanity is doing the same thing over and over and expecting different results—then my efforts at Internet dating were clearly indicative of madness.

Blame it on love. Love can do that to you—it can make you nuts.

Actually, I take that back. It's not love that makes people nuts. It's the absence of love. It's the fear of losing love. And in my case—under Franklin's definition—it was the search for love, a search for something so reputedly desirable that I willingly and repeatedly endured a process that any empiricist would conclude was futile.

Then again, when did Benjamin Franklin become an expert on love? Sure, he knew a thing or two about democracy, and apparently he was pretty good with a kite, but one needn't read more than a page or two of *Poor Richard's Almanac* to realize that Franklin was no Nicholas Sparks. Maybe, when it comes to searching for love, continuing the quest despite repeated failure is not a sign of insanity. Maybe, instead, one who quixotically presses on in pursuit of love is more akin to the determined lottery player, the one who bets on the same numbers week after week, aware that the odds are long, but aware, too, that to have any chance at winning, one must keep on placing the bet. Is the lottery player optimistic? Of course. Foolishly so? Perhaps. But insane? No.

And neither was I. Not yet, at least. Yes, I was discouraged, and yes, I was tired. I'll even admit that as the number of my first dates climbed to more than 90, I found myself frequently seized with an impulse to hurl my computer out the window in a liberating "I quit!" gesture to the entire process. Deep down, though, I simply was not ready to concede. Despite all the repetition and failure, despite the consistently zero yield on my substantial investment of time and energy, I was not yet ready to give up the hope of finding an enduring love, nor was I ready to surrender the initiative that Internet dating afforded—maddening though the process may have been.

Instead, I did something that no smart lottery player would ever do: I bet on a different set of numbers.

Bad idea.

* * *

In my several years of Internet dating, I'd been reasonably open-minded about the women I chose to pursue. If I liked the look of a woman's photos and the way she expressed herself in her essays, I'd write to her whether she was divorced, separated, widowed, or never married, whether she did or did not have children, whether she was blonde, brunette, redhead, or any combination of all three. I dated women of different ethnicities, different faiths, and different nationalities. I went out with women at every educational level, from those with no more than high school diplomas to those with post-graduate degrees, and I cared little about whether a woman was career-minded or a stay-at-home mom. From the beginning of my online dating, I'd refused to limit myself to women who met the specs of some narrow, perfect-match wish list, believing, instead, that love is sneakier than all that, with a penchant for arriving unexpectedly and circuitously, and that to accommodate an unexpected, circuitous arrival I had to open as many doors and windows as possible.

Up to now, though, I'd respected a particular numerical boundary. Despite all the sophomoric, lecherous prodding of many of my long-married male friends (who simply couldn't understand why I wasn't out there sampling what they imagined to be an inexhaustible bounty of 29-year-old sex kittens), I'd confined my online search to women who fit within a certain age range—anywhere from eight years younger than I, to two years older. My reasoning wasn't necessarily rational or inarguable—it was just that a ten-year age range seemed to me to be generationally appropriate.

Well, perhaps it was. But so what? For all my generational propriety, here I sat, unattached, unconnected, and as yet unacquainted with any woman who could inspire in me a spark of infatuation lasting more than eight or nine weeks. Given the generally broad array of age-appropriate women I'd pursued thus far, and given my undeniable lack of success, maybe I needed to widen my options—stretch my numerical boundary—by expanding the age range of my search. Sure, the thought of a man in his early forties dating a woman in her late twenties has a bit of a robbing-the-cradle feel to it, but if the man is now in his late forties (I was, by now, 48), and the woman is no younger than 35, it doesn't sound nearly as wrong, does it?

* * *

Not surprisingly, when a man is 48, attracting the interest of a 35-year-old woman is appreciably more difficult than attracting the interest of a woman in her early forties. (Erin was 35 when we first started dating, but I was only 42 at the time.) The profiles of women in their mid to late thirties revealed that most of them very sensibly sought a mate whose age, relative to their own, was anywhere from two years younger to six or seven years older. Occasionally, I'd happen upon profiles in which the age range was broader—in which the women were amenable to inquiries from men who were eight years older, or even ten years older—but locating an appealing woman in her mid-thirties who was open to an age difference of more than ten years was proving to be extraordinarily difficult. Finally, though, on one particular evening, after dozens of misses, I hit upon the profile of an adorable 35-year-old whose desired age range shouted out at me like a cheerleader with a megaphone: 40 to 50!

Of course, I was not unaware of the fact that sometimes, when a woman is open to romance with a man nearly fifty percent older than she is, she may be wrestling with a serious "daddy" issue or two. Daddy issues can be trouble in a romance, and I was determined, therefore, to be careful. But consistent with my open-door, open-window philosophy, I resisted the temptation to prejudge. An assumption is nothing more than an educated guess, and an educated guess is, still, just a guess. Why guess about whether this adorable 35-year-old was plagued by debilitating daddy issues when, with a modicum of patience and effort, I could actually know for sure.

Her name was Jordan, and she arrived for our first date—casual drinks on a Tuesday night at a local sports bar (her choice)—in blue jeans and an oversized sweater, with unbanded cuffs that hung loosely down at her fingertips. Even lovelier in person than in her pictures, she had a bashful yet cuddly manner that seemed to say, "Please, hug me"—childlike, in a way, although perhaps my heightened sensitivity to the difference in our ages had me seeing things that weren't really there.

For two hours, over two beers and lots of small talk, she revealed the basics. She was born in New York, where she lived with her doctor father and her homemaker mother until leaving for college at the age of 17. She received a degree in nursing, then worked as an RN in Baltimore for a

162

decade before moving to Boca Raton, where for the past three or four years she'd worked as an OR nurse at a local hospital. Never married, with no kids, she'd had three long-term relationships, each spanning two or three years (more or less), but each, sadly, marred by abuse, both verbal and physical.

"I'm really shitty at picking the right guy," she explained, "and even worse at knowing how to get out of bad situations." Despite the fact that she was always on the receiving end of the abuse, all three relationships ended with the boyfriend leaving her.

"That's why I decided to look for an older guy," she continued. "I'm thinking maybe I just need to be with someone more stable and mature."

Her life's path seemed puzzling to me—when a woman falls into a pattern of abusive relationships, something is amiss, regardless of how bright and lovely she may be, and regardless of her two-parent, upper-middle-class background—but perhaps the explanation was no more complicated than a run of supremely rotten luck. I wasn't quite sure whether she and I had any potential together, nor was I clear about whether the warmth I was feeling toward her was a sign of attraction, sympathy, or some fatherly instinct to want to salve her wounds, but this was only our first date. I had some time to sort it all out.

It wouldn't take long.

* * *

We were sitting outdoors on our second date, awaiting our salads at a bistro-style café.

"I really enjoy talking to you," she said. "You're so calm, and you make me feel like you're really listening to what I'm saying."

"Well, thank you," I said. "But why wouldn't I be calm? And why wouldn't I be listening to what you're saying?"

"I don't know," she said, "I'm just not used to that."

I *was* listening. I was listening very attentively. Purposefully or not, Jordan was telling me quite a lot about herself, and not because I was asking. Apparently she'd been storing things up for some time now—thoughts, stories, feelings, fears—just waiting for someone to come along who might be willing to pay attention.

Her childhood, as it turns out, was less than rosy, and since my antenna had already been searching for signals, I was not at all surprised when she began to detail a somewhat chilly relationship with her father. Her story was sad but not necessarily unusual—despite all her different efforts throughout the varying stages of her youth, she simply couldn't get her father to show anything more than an obligatory, passing interest in any aspect of her life—but the more she talked, the more I could feel not just her sadness, but her sense of yearning. She'd always assumed her father's distance was attributable to some inadequacy on her part, and she'd been trying (and failing), her entire life, to figure out what that was. I felt like saying, "Jordan, it had nothing to do with you—your father was just an asshole," but if I'd learned anything from my years of therapy, it was not to interrupt someone who was tapping into the depths of inner turmoil.

"I can't believe I'm telling you all this stuff," she said, "but it's just that you're so easy to talk to."

I thanked her again, assuring her that everyone has a story to tell. "So don't think," I said, "that you're burdening me by telling me yours."

"Yeah," she said, "but most people's stories don't have as much bad stuff as mine."

"Oh, I don't know," I responded, "I've heard stories much worse than yours."

"Maybe," she said, "but I haven't told you any of the really bad stuff yet."

Hmm, I thought, this poor woman is definitely harboring some kind of pain, and is clearly seeking some type of relief.

"So tell me the bad parts," I said.

She hesitated, sizing me up for a second or two with a half-coy, half-nervous, half-sideways grin, before asking, "If I tell you all the really bad stuff, will you promise not to get up and run out of here?"

"Sure," I replied, "I promise."

"Okay," she said, and then, without any further segue or fanfare, and with very little emotion, she dropped her first real bombshell.

"My father had a friend," she said, "who started molesting me when I was four years old."

* * *

I'm not a physically imposing fellow, and I'm proud of the fact that in all my years as an adult, I've never been involved in a physical altercation with anyone. I'm completely unashamed of my belief that cutting and running, whenever possible, is almost always preferable to getting one's nose bloodied. But as Jordan went on, I could feel the muscles tighten in my neck and jaw, and my hands start to curl into fists. As a father, as a man, as a human being, the thought of any adult preying sexually on a four-year-old child was enough to make me acknowledge the rare virtue of violence. Jordan, on the other hand, remained generously calm.

"His name was Frank," she continued, "but he was my dad's best friend, so I was always told to call him Uncle Frank. Whenever he was over, he would come into my room with a pack of M&Ms, and he would give me some of the M&Ms if I would do things to him or let him do things to me. You know, two M&Ms for this, three M&Ms for that—that kind of thing."

"Didn't you tell your parents," I asked, as calmly as I could, trying hard to hide the extent of my growing anger for fear that too extreme a reaction might inhibit Jordan from continuing.

"Not at first," she said. "Remember, I was only four years old when it started. I thought it was like a game. Plus, he was Uncle Frank—if he was asking me to do these things, how could they be wrong? But by the time I was eight, I started to feel like something was not right about it, and that's when I told my parents."

"So what happened?" I asked.

"My father got furious. " she said.

"Good!" I barked.

"No," she interrupted, "not good. His fury was directed at me. He screamed at me, calling me a liar, and shouting that if I ever again said such horrible things about Uncle Frank, he'd spank me so hard I would never stop crying."

I could not get my brain to connect to my jaw, could not coherently turn my thoughts into words. "That's...that's just...it's...unbelievable," I stammered, livid at what I was hearing, livid that any parent—any human—could be so monstrous. "What did your mother do?"

"She just stood there," she said, "while he screamed at me."

All I could do was gasp.

*　*　*

For the rest of the evening, in my mind's eye, Jordan was no longer a date, and I was no longer a single male seeking romance—she was a child, and I was a father offering comfort. Yes, of course, in the abstract I'd seen it coming, and no, of course, I had no interest in the further development of such a twisted relationship. But for the rest of that evening, until Jordan had released as many secrets and demons as her wounded psyche would allow, I was not about to abandon this poor child in need of some warmth. Chapter by chapter, the unfiltered details of Jordan's thirty-five years spilled out of her, and bit by bit, pieces of my heart—the heart of a father—were breaking.

Her story had all the elements of the classic abused child cliché, and if I saw the various vignettes of her life as a coming attraction for some movie, I'd be sure to put the movie in the "don't bother" column of my must-see list. I've seen that film a hundred times already. We all have. But Jordan was a flesh-and-blood human being, and when the star of the movie is sitting before you, recounting it all in the first person, the story is no longer a cliché.

She did, in fact, move to North Carolina at 17, although not to go to college—she'd make her way to nursing school 10 years later—but, instead, to get away from the cesspool she knew as home. Rebelling from her upper-middle-class upbringing (and who could blame her), she fell in with what she described as a "seedy" crowd, moving from one violent relationship to the next (including a six-month lesbian affair with a woman she described as "a 53-year-old bull dyke"), all the while dancing at strip clubs to earn a living.

The incongruity of the moment was striking. In the safe and gentle cocoon of a courtyard bistro on a warm and balmy Florida night, a sweet, bright, adorable woman was calmly, almost matter-of-factly sharing with me the details of what, to me, could only be described as a living nightmare. Violence? Abuse? Strip clubs? Affairs with partners more than thirty years older? I was no hermit, but these were not of my world. Strangely, though, while my anger and outrage ballooned with each twist and turn in her harrowing narrative, Jordan betrayed no sense of rage or fury at all. Whether she'd repressed her accumulated pain into a numbed state of disaffection, or simply had not experienced enough of the alternative to know that she should have been burning with anger, I couldn't tell. Clearly, though, despite the relatively stoic manner in which she was conveying her tale, she was nevertheless conveying it without hesitation, and I was not about to do or say anything that would interfere with such an obviously needed release.

She'd had two dreams as a child—one was to work in the medical field (no surprise, considering her constant efforts at winning her physician father's affections), and one was to be married and raise a family. To her credit, she'd achieved the former; to her dismay, she'd been failing at the latter.

Obtaining her nursing degree was the easy part, relatively speaking. Her dancing years had been lucrative, and despite the seamy environment, the violent boyfriends, and the ubiquitous temptations of drugs and alcohol, she'd managed her money well. Her parents had provided no support throughout her years away from home, but by the time she reached her late twenties she'd put enough money away, on her own, both to pay for nursing school and to support herself at the same time.

She loved nursing school, and she loved the nursing profession as a career. She especially loved the more professional, more educated people—particularly the men—to whom the health care world had exposed her, and from her earliest days in the nursing program she'd developed what she thought was a realistic hope of achieving her second dream— of meeting a marriage-worthy, professional man and raising a family of her own. She did, in fact, meet several men throughout her nursing school years, as well as in the few years since—men who fit the image of what she'd want in a husband and a family man—but two things consistently interfered with her ability to turn any of those encounters into the realization of her dream.

The first was what she described as an inexplicable aversion to kissing on the lips. "It's just always grossed me out," she said, "and I can't figure out why it's such a big deal to guys. I'm fine with any kind of sex, I just don't like kissing on the lips."

I just shook my head and listened.

The second problem, she said, was the tougher one—a problem understandably troublesome to men, but one she'd been unable to fix.

She couldn't give up the stripping.

* * *

Her stage name as a dancer was "Nevada," a name she'd selected for no reason other than she liked the way it sounded.

"I quit the dancing when I started nursing school," she said, "and I never expected to go back. But after about three months, I just needed it." Pantomiming the gesture of a junkie holding a syringe, she tapped her arm, explaining, "It was like my fix."

"How so?" I asked.

169

"I don't know," she said, "it's almost like I'm two different people. When I'm Jordan, I'm mostly miserable, but when I'm Nevada, it's like I'm in a totally separate place— I put on my outfits and I get up on the stage, and everyone loves me, and the bouncers and the crew, they all protect me, and the girls are all my friends, and the music is playing, and everyone's having a good time . . ."

She paused for a few seconds, looking off reflectively. I said nothing, letting the silence, at that moment, provide its own encouragement.

"I guess part of what's so great about it," she continued, "is that when I'm up there as Nevada, I know that everyone loves me, but no one can hurt me."

I nodded.

"And every once in a while," she said, "I just need to feel that way."

Yes, she answered, in response to what was probably an obvious question—yes, she'd been to counseling. Recently. Her health insurance covered three visits, and she very much enjoyed her sessions, but since she'd used her savings to cover the nursing school years, she was in no position financially to pay for more therapy on her own—she earned far less as a nurse than she'd earned as a stripper, and her part-time dancing provided little more than spending money. At the end of her third session—her last—she asked the therapist whether he thought she should stop the dancing.

"He said I shouldn't stop," she said. "He said that he didn't think I was strong enough to give it up just yet."

And so Jordan's plan was to continue her periodic appearances at a local strip club, where, as "Nevada," for a two or three night stretch each time, she would get her needed fix of pain-free love. She knew that her stripping compulsion was a death knell to the picket-fence life of her dreams. She just couldn't kick the habit.

* * *

We stood at her car to part ways for the night. "I'm sure you'll never want to see me again," she said. "And with all the shit you heard tonight, who could blame you?"

I responded with one truth, one half-truth, and one lie.

The truth was acknowledging that we wouldn't be seeing each other again. The absolute impossibility of any romantic involvement with Jordan had been clear to me for hours. On so many obvious levels it was simply out of the question, and despite my sympathy for her, my anger toward her parents, and my reflexive protective instincts, I could not permit myself to be sucked in to any rescue project, let alone one as hopeless as hers.

The half-truth was offering a less negative reason for declining to pursue things further.

"It would be silly for us to continue," I said "We each want such different things. You're 35. You're young. You want to have children and a family and to live that whole start-to-finish family life. I've done that already. I'm practically an empty-nester, and I don't plan on starting another family. You deserve to have what you want, and you could never have that with me. Taking this any further just wouldn't be fair to you."

"I know," she said, "I know. It's just that as more and more time goes by, I start to feel like there's less and less of a chance that I'll ever find what I really want."

"Oh, that's nonsense," I said. "Don't give up. You've come so far. You'll find it."

That last part was the lie.

* * *

I didn't sleep that night, and I remained in a funk for most of the next day, wracked with a frustrating combination of sadness and powerlessness. Of all my dates over the past several years—of all the different stories from all the different women—none left me feeling so disturbed. She had that rare combination of brains, beauty, pluck, and charisma—a combination that, in another household, with another set of parents, could have formed the foundation for a charmed existence. Instead, she'd been crushed—consigned forever into that void between desperately wanting some version of normality and being permanently unable to accept it—and neither I, nor anyone else, would ever be able to do anything about it. I'd been on the lookout for daddy issues. What I'd discovered, instead, were daddy crimes. It made me sick.

As dinnertime approached, and with my funk unabated, my mother called. It was a Sunday, and she was calling as part of her normal Sunday routine, just to see how my weekend had gone.

Still lightning-quick in her mid-seventies, my mother is a very funny woman, with an almost professional sense of comedic timing, so I should have expected that she would figure out the perfect line, at the perfect time, to snap me out of my foul mood.

I had just finished sharing with her all the pathetic, frustrating, anger-inducing details of the prior night's date with Jordan: The abuse by Uncle Frank, the disgraceful reaction of her parents, the running away from home, the violent men, the 53-year-old bull dyke, the aversion to kissing, the stripping—I left out nothing.

From the other end of the line—silence.

One second passed.

Two seconds.

172

Three seconds.

Four seconds.

Then, finally, with the tension from the silence growing thick and heavy, my mother, in a voice that contained not a hint of shock or displeasure, said ever so sweetly and calmly:

"So when are you seeing her again?"

PART THREE

CULMINATION

CHAPTER THIRTEEN—IT WASN'T ME

I know her.

She's 43 years old, with two children, both in high school. Her devotion to her kids is genuine and selfless—and it shows. Though not immune to the difficult but healthy emotional ups and downs so typical of the late teen years, her children display all the markers—all the kindness, caring, and responsibility—that so often point to attentive, dedicated parenting. I admire her for that.

She has a masters degree in interior architecture, and works from her house doing residential interior design, but she has a passion and a talent for painting—oils, mostly—and while she loves her work, she fantasizes about the day, in the not-too-distant future, when she can spend more time painting and less time designing.

She likes Chet Baker, the violin concertos of Giuseppe Tartini, and Paul McCartney singing "Maybe I'm Amazed." Whether eating out or eating in, she likes a glass of wine with dinner, but her social drink of choice is a Grey Goose martini, dirty. She's petite, trim, and in very good shape, although her overall fitness is more the product of a moderate, thoughtful lifestyle than any fanatical exercise regimen. She's into yoga and meditation, but she's decidedly not religious. She's beautiful, of course, although it's a beauty resulting not so much from any classic facial bone structure as from the clarity in her eyes and the ease in her smile.

She loves to travel, but when she travels she loves not just the running and doing and seeing—although she loves that a lot—but also just the feeling of being somewhere different, of spending a day or a week in a faraway place with no plan or agenda, just taking in the scents and the sounds, and acquiring, through her pores, an overall sensation of what this new and unfamiliar place is all about.

She reads avidly—fiction, nonfiction, newspapers, magazines—and she loves almost every genre of movie. She likes crossword puzzles and board games, art shows and craft fairs, and concerts of any type. She had violin lessons as a child, knows her way around a piano keyboard, and while she's not much of a sports enthusiast, she's always noticed and appreciated a certain pastoral poetry in the rhythm and the feel of a game of baseball.

She was married for thirteen years, has been single, now, for six, and has realized, through the passage of time and with the benefit of experience, that when it comes to love and sex, she has no shortage of desires, but very few needs. While she'd be thrilled to discover a hot, soulful, juicy, heavy, deep, caring, tender, loving, meaningful relationship, she's not out there hunting it down like a starving cat in search of a meal. If she crosses paths with romance, she'll happily take the journey. And if her road remains alone, that's okay, too. She has a dog.

She's the woman I've been looking for.

I love her.

She doesn't exist.

* * *

Months would pass before I'd realize that my dinner with Jordan marked the start of a certain downward shift in my typical first-date mindset, a shift that was not simply part of a regular cycle of burnout, but more a descent into a state of resignation. Eventually I'd realize how that evening, in its own stark way, encapsulated all the futility of the past several years, and how the combination of that futility and the darkness of Jordan's tale tilted the outlook with which I approached each subsequent first-date—tilted it away from the hopeful "maybe this is the one that'll last," toward a more defeatist "let's find out what's wrong with this one." Gradually, I'd connect the dots leading back from Jordan to my very first post-marital date—the "wrong woman" with whom Helen Eisenberg first set me up—and I'd shake my head at the irony of how every woman since then has likewise, for one reason or another, been "wrong." That dinner with Jordan was a turning point for me, although months would pass before I'd comprehend how sharp a turn it really was.

In the interim, I continued to date—four different Ilenes, three different Debbies, a three-in-a-row string of Shelly, Sheri, and Shari—and while not all of the women, after meeting me, had a desire to pursue anything further, for the ones who did, always, as predictably as the rising of the sun, a blatant disqualifier would ultimately surface, bringing things to an early end. There was the woman who, having invited me into her bed on our second date, turned to me in the afterglow and asked, in all seriousness, "So, is your house big enough for me and my kids?" There was the woman who, midway through our first date, started calling me "Pookie," and who, the very next day, phoned me seven times—seven times!—at my office, just to let me know she was thinking about me. There was the never-married woman who'd been living in the same apartment for 10 years without putting a single picture on a wall—ten years surrounded by nothing but stark, white paint—because she assumed she'd eventually meet someone and move out, so why bother?

Like a circular, never-ending roller coaster, the dates continued, one after another after another, with my boxcar repeatedly cresting that short but inevitable arc from hope to

179

disappointment, from "maybe this time" to "get me out of here."

It wasn't me. Each time one of these deal-breaking incidents would occur, I'd share the details with my shrink and my closest friends, and in each instance everyone would agree. It wasn't me. A woman who, after a second date, would ask about moving in—with kids, no less!—should be avoided. A woman who, after a single date—or ever, for that matter—would call your office seven times in one day, should be feared. A woman who would postpone the actual living of a life for more than ten years while waiting for her fantasy prince to arrive should be studied—but by scientists, not by me.

No, it wasn't me. While hardly without my own flaws and quirks, my refusal during these past several years to walk a permanent path with any of the prospects I'd encountered could not be attributed to my own defects or eccentricities. My aversion to women with more facial hair than I was not unreasonable. My objection to women who've slept with more than 100 men was not unusual. My disdain for women who've given up sex forever was not boorish. My inability to feel a physical attraction for women twice my weight was not uncommon. My decision to end a relationship with a woman who was asking me to act other than in the best interests of my children was not foolish. I had no humanistic responsibility to accept involvement with women who had eating disorders, or contagious diseases, or who were incapable of orgasms, or who wanted to sleep with other women, or who lived comfortably amid filth, or who called me "Pookie"—on a first date!

It wasn't me.

I was trying. I was out there. I was enduring the coffee, enduring the cocktails, enduring the interminable butt-sniffing, but not because butt-sniffing is particularly appealing or enjoyable, and not because of any masochistic fondness for ass fumes. I endured it all—all the redundancy, all the profiles and e-mails and phone calls, all the house wine and sauceless mahi-mahi—in the good faith belief that to find a diamond in the rough, one must be willing to spend a substantial amount of time actually in the rough. But at what point—after how much time—can one conclude without fear of being hasty that the rough is in fact bereft of gems, and is filled to the brim, instead, with nothing but rough, rough, and more rough?

Oh, sure, there's my "one in two hundred" construct, and since the number of my first dates climbed past the 100 mark shortly after my dinner with Jordan, one could argue that I should quit my belly-aching and just keep on going— that I was already more than halfway toward my goal of finding an enduring love. But who's to say that I'm right about "one in two hundred?" I made that up. It was just a guess. What if I'm wrong? What if it's not "one in two hundred?" What if it's "one in five hundred," or "one in a thousand?" Besides, "one in two hundred" seems so painlessly attainable only because it sounds so much less challenging than the more familiar "one in a million," but when you realize that saying "one in two hundred" is the same as saying one-half of one percent, you can start to panic over whether you've analyzed the construct correctly. I mean, I'm neither a statistician nor a handicapper, but does my "one in two hundred" construct mean that if I meet two hundred different women, I will definitely find a love with *at least* one of them? Or does it mean that no matter how many women I meet, I stand only a one-half of one percent chance of finding a lasting love with *any* one of them?

These are questions without definitive answers, but after dates with more than 100 women over a period spanning not just months but years—after hundreds of pages of e-mail, thousands of hours on the phone, dozens upon dozens of cappuccinos and lattés—after sampling every bar, bistro, patisserie, and café in a tri-county area—after small-talking my way through an ever-repeating gauntlet of brunches, lunches, dinners, and desserts, all in an unrestrained, spare-no-effort, leave-no-rock-unturned campaign for love—I can definitively say this about my failure thus far:

It wasn't me.

CHAPTER FOURTEEN—IT'S ME

It's me.

* * *

No, I'm not gay—nor would I even feel a need to address the issue had not one of my married male friends, in all his oafish glory, brought it up.

My married male friends tend to see my singlehood through a prismatic lens—a lens that, depending on the angle of view, can make the same subject appear blue one second, red the next. Viewing my unattached life at one angle, my married male friends all tend to envy me—they envy my freedom, they envy my easygoing lifestyle, and, of course, they envy that I've had such variety in my interactions with the opposite sex. But skew the angle of view slightly, and those same friends, viewing the same objective conditions, tend to see my circumstances differently—instead of envying my freedom, they feel sorry that I'm not part of a couple; instead of envying my easygoing lifestyle, they feel sorry for my solitary existence; instead of envying the variety of my social life, they feel sorry for the superficiality of my relationships.

When the angle of the prism is tilted toward envy, my married male friends tend to shift into receptor mode, with all of them wanting me to regale them with my tales of single life—the more salacious, the better—so they can vicariously enjoy what they imagine to be a world of non-stop adventure and fun. But when the angle of the prism is tilted toward sympathy, those same friends tend to shift into dispenser mode, with most of them wanting to dole out their sage advice on how I might free myself from what they imagine to be such an empty, soulless rut.

In truth, my life is neither—it's neither a non-stop world of adventure and fun, nor an empty, soulless rut—but since none of my married male friends has ever been a single, middle-aged man (they've all been married since their early twenties), even the really smart ones, for all their good intentions, have difficulty getting a handle on what my life is all about—which, in turn, tends to lead to some ridiculously out-of-touch advice. And so when my good friend, David—who's not even one of the really smart ones—came to me in dispenser mode at a party one night, I expected no epiphanies.

David's always been a loyal and well-meaning friend, but he's not a particularly deep thinker, nor is he known for possessing an especially useful inventory of wisdom. He's the kind of guy who'll drive too fast over the same speed bump, day after day, each time cursing, "Damn, I have to remember that's there!" So when he pulled me aside saying he had some thoughts about why I'd been failing at long-term love, I expected mostly drivel—and I got what I expected. Mostly.

"I've been thinking about it long and hard," he started, which I'm sure he believed, but which, knowing David, was simply not possible, "and here's what I think. I think it has nothing to do with the women. I think it's you. I think you're gay."

Given David's limited capacity for serious thought, his final conclusion was not surprising. In his simplistic, "either/or" slant on life, a man either lives with a woman, or he's gay, and while, for a time, he gave me the benefit of the doubt—"Hey," he would say, "a guy's entitled to a few post-divorce single years, just to fool around"—in his mind that time had expired. I'd been divorced for several years, and I was still alone. For David, there was only one plausible explanation. End of story.

Ironically, if he'd ended his statement just before its well-meaning but shallow conclusion—if he'd ended at the "I think it's you" part—he'd have been the first of my friends to verbalize a notion I'd only recently begun to explore for myself.

"No, David," I said, "I'm not gay. But I've been thinking long and hard about it, too. And for a lot of other reasons, I think you may have gotten part of it right."

* * *

Let's face it: I've spent the better part of my 40s on this love-seeking odyssey, but at each of my many opportunities, I've chosen either not to pursue, or not to continue, a particular romance. Yes, I can rant on and on, convincingly, about the correctness of each of my decisions, and when each decision is considered in isolation, one would be hard-pressed to come up with a rational argument as to why any of those decisions was wrong. But who am I kidding? When I look back at the totality and the consistency of those decisions—when I tabulate the sheer volume of opportunities afforded me, then add my persistent unwillingness to settle on even one of them—I see an equation that resolves at only one conclusion.

It's hard to argue with the math.

It must have something to do with me.

* * *

On any journey, time creates distance, and with distance comes perspective—the ability to see the big picture. When I look at the big picture of my past several years I see a layered landscape, a landscape in which all the Noras and Erins and Bonnies and Alisons have been painted with the brush of my own foibles and biases. It's a landscape that both depicts and reveals. It depicts the women. It reveals me.

It reveals my impatience—my impetuous proclivity to conclude within minutes of meeting a woman that she either is or is not worthy of a more substantial investment of time and emotion. It reveals my intolerance—my snobbish inclination to look down my nose at a woman merely because she writes about being an "optomist" instead of an "optimist." It reveals my rigidity—my stubborn unwillingness to remain involved with a woman who exhibits any trait or tendency that falls even slightly outside my own arbitrary comfort zone. Viewed from a particular distance, the landscape of my past several years reveals layers of self-induced, often neurotically-inspired decisions and behaviors, each of which has interfered materially with any chance of realizing my own stated desire for a deep and lasting love.

The shrinks would say those decisions and behaviors are indicative of self-loathing—that my biases are actually projections of what I dislike about myself—and that since I subconsciously believe I'm not worthy of being loved, I subconsciously sabotage any chance at love through those decisions and behaviors that foreclose the possibility.

I have too much respect for psychology, and I've invested too much money into my own therapy over the years, to deny that the theory makes sense. I buy it. I'm sure, in my case, the whole "self-loathing" concept explains a lot, and I'm working on it. But when I look at the big picture from just a few more steps back, I see yet another layer on the landscape, a layer at which all my decisions and behaviors, all my foibles and biases, coalesce into a broader picture as a whole, a picture that provides an additional explanation for what's preventing me from falling into a deep and lasting love.

It's a picture filled with fear.

Or, to put it another way: I'm scared shitless.

* * *

Long-term love requires a certain sacrifice of self, a surrender of a piece of one's individuality, in exchange for the benefits of couplehood. When we're young—when we fall in love in our twenties—the surrender is minimal, and the benefits are significant. We're barely out of adolescence, with our adult personas far from full maturity, so we're hardly aware of the sacrifice we're making. Yet our primordial instincts toward procreation in general, as well as our societal inclinations toward the creation and maintenance of a family unit, are at full force, fomenting and exerting innate pressures for which the environment of couplehood provides an acceptable and ready release. By providing for something we instinctively and urgently crave, and requiring only, in exchange, that we sacrifice something we don't yet fully possess, long-term love—when we're young—is a very good deal.

But when that youthful long-term love ends at divorce in middle-age, a profound transformation can occur, one that can alter the deal's dynamics substantially—and not for the better.

While there are those who jump rapidly into new, traditional, living-under-one-roof relationships, some of us who married in our barely-post-pubescent twenties, and who find ourselves newly divorced in our worldlier, more mature forties, are not so quick to take another plunge. Whether resulting from choice or the absence of opportunity, we adapt, little by little, to the strangeness of singlehood, until gradually, over a period of two or three years, we find that we've climbed our way to a comfortably elevated state of independence.

It's an accomplishment—an appreciation for a level of self-hood one had neither achieved before getting married, nor had any opportunity to experience until after getting divorced. It's a feeling of wholeness that sneaks up on you, building almost imperceptibly during those first few post-divorce years while you flounder and struggle for your footing, but rising within you nevertheless, until one day, as your lover of the moment is pushing you back toward a sharing-the-same-garage version of couplehood, you catch yourself thinking: Hey, wait a minute, it took so long for me to reach this point, this sense of satisfaction and contentment with myself—I'm not so sure I want to give that up.

At the same time, when you're divorced and in your forties, those fundamental imperatives to procreate and establish family units—imperatives that found their easy response within the socially acceptable walls of couplehood—no longer exert much pull. To the contrary—in middle age, when you and your lover each have children of your own, forging a new, combined family unit can often be more struggle than joy, especially when those children are in their teens.

Of course, some people—for financial reasons, emotional reasons, or otherwise—will always prefer couplehood, regardless of the sacrifice or the struggle. For others, though—for those whose financial and emotional resources can withstand the requirements of single life, and who cherish and value their newly achieved autonomy—the thought of sacrificing an elevated state of independence for a relationship likely to involve more struggle than joy seems not merely foolish, it seems downright perilous.

It scares the crap out of me.

But that's not what scares me the most.

* * *

The woman I married when I was 24 years old—and to whom I remained married for 17 years—was bright (first in her class at graduate school), beautiful (prom queen at her high school), and good-hearted (founder of a local feed-the-hungry campaign that continues to this day, and is named in her memory). Through the course of our 17 married years together we produced two remarkable children, developed dozens of cherished friendships, contributed countless hours and dollars toward the betterment of our community, and were considered by many to be the very model of what a happy, loving couple should be. But of course, as happens with most models, when the sheen of our public face was removed—when we were sheltered behind the privacy of our own closed doors—a more true-to-life image emerged, an image hardly as appealing or as enviable as the one we presented to our family, our friends, and our community. The sad, secret fact—the truth that no one knew—was that sometime during our first few years, the love just went away. And with it went all the warmth, all the tenderness, all the humor of our happier days, replaced instead with a harsh, laughless, distant chill—a chill unnoticed by anyone, not even our children, because it befell us only when the doors were closed and we were locked inside, alone.

Toward the very end of our listless marriage, I had an affair—an affair that some would see as predictable given the state of our marriage at the time, but which, predictable or not, was wrong—and while the affair was not the cause of the end of the marriage, it certainly didn't make the divorce any easier. The emotional emptiness of our waning marital years was a closed-door secret my wife and I had been keeping to ourselves, but when our marriage ended, it ended badly, in a crush of acrimony and sorrow so heavy and vast it spared no one within our little corner of the world—not my wife, not my kids, not our families or our friends, not me—no one. In our divorce, everyone got hurt—and the pain was categorically wicked.

Love starts pretty. It ends ugly. And the thought of going through that again—the thought of enduring the trauma of another hideous end—fills me with a fear that's close to paralyzing.

But that, too, is not what scares me the most. What scares me the most is not that love ends ugly.

What scares me the most is that love ends at all.

CHAPTER FIFTEEN—WHAT IS LOVE?

A movie starts, and within the first five minutes, the writer and the director, through the skillful manipulation of words, images, and camera angles, have set the premise: Man "A" is married to woman "A." They have kids. They're not happy. Woman "B" is married to man "B." They, too, have kids and are not happy. The couples have never before met, but through some accident of timing and circumstance, man "A" encounters woman "B," a cute verbal exchange occurs, eyes lock for a millisecond longer than the usual social protocols would allow, and, presto—we, the audience, for the next ninety minutes, will suspend all notions of fealty and propriety, and root, instead, for the union of man "A" and woman "B." Forget that such a coming together requires the breakup of two families. Forget that, years earlier, couple "A" and couple "B" probably got their separate starts through similarly romantic chance encounters. And forget that the budding relationship for which we're now rooting is as likely to fail as the time-scarred relationship it's intended to replace. When the promise of love is dangled before us, we root for love regardless. Love isn't blind. It's blinding.

* * *

A few weeks after my wife and I separated, I received a comfort call from one of our neighbors. About ten years older than I, Doug was married to Sandy—his third marriage, her second. As couples, we'd socialized maybe half-a-dozen times during the five or six years since we'd first become acquainted, but the socializing, while always pleasant, never quite progressed into full-fledged friendship. We were friendly neighbors, but nothing more than friendly neighbors, and so I was somewhat surprised by Doug's call.

191

"Hey, man," he said, in a sympathetic voice, "I heard about the separation, and I'd like to buy you a beer if you're free one night this week."

Doug had never been one of my confidantes, and I'd already done plenty of gut-spilling about the separation, over plenty of beers, with plenty of good, close friends. But when you're newly separated after a long-term marriage, the spillage flows constantly, and you never turn down another opportunity to drain your emotions over a drink—even if it's with someone who's more neighbor than friend.

My expectation, as I met up with him the next night at a local bar and grill, was that Doug would ask few if any probing questions, would listen politely and supportively to as much as I chose to tell him, and would end the evening by picking up the tab and offering to "be there" for anything I might need during the stressful days ahead. That was pretty much the standard script for any post-separation, sorrow-drowning, weeknight beer-drinking session with the guys, and Doug's invitation gave me no reason to believe he'd be deviating even one iota from that script.

Maybe, if I'd known him better, I'd have been less surprised at his capacity to ad lib.

* * *

"Listen," he started, immediately, before the first round of beers had been ordered, and without even asking me how I was doing, "I'm sure, for you to leave, things must have been pretty bad between the two of you, but I've been through this a couple of times myself, and before you make the separation permanent, I've got to let you in on one of life's little secrets."

Excuse me? This isn't supposed to happen. This isn't supposed to be about life's little secrets. Doug's not supposed to be doing any real talking. This is supposed to be about Doug just sitting there for two hours, shaking his head, and offering the occasional, "Yeah, I know what you mean," or, "Yeah, but don't worry, you'll get through it." I hadn't even said anything yet. Why was he speaking?

"Just order a beer, sit back, and listen to me," he said. "And trust me—I know what I'm talking about."

"Um, okay," I muttered, clearly disarmed by his unorthodox, aggressive approach, but also somewhat curious, and maybe even a bit amused. "So what's the little secret?"

"Relax," he said, as he gestured for the waitress, "we'll get to it."

* * *

For two hours over five beers (four for him, one for me), I listened as Doug took me on a somewhat inebriated tour of his three marriages.

Felice was his first wife. They met and fell in love in their last year of college, got married two years later, had their first daughter, Wendy, just before their second anniversary, and their second daughter, Emily, a year-and-a-half later. Emily was an accident—"We were already headed downhill after Wendy, although please don't ask me why, because I have no fucking idea"—and things just got progressively worse after that. They split up before Emily's first birthday.

He vowed after his divorce from Felice that if ever he fell in love again, he'd wait a good deal longer before committing to a marriage, just to be sure that the love didn't wither. A year later, he fell in love with Joanie, but five years would pass before she'd become his second wife—five years in which the steady, unrelenting growth of his affection for her ultimately convinced him that this was a love for the ages.

"I'd probably still be married to her today," he said, "had I not come home early one night to find her face buried between the open legs of our housekeeper, Iolanda."

Ouch.

Doug swore off love for good after Joanie, spending the next few years in a series of shallow, meaningless relationships that were short on intimacy, long on sex, and brief in duration. Then someone fixed him up with Sandy, and...Pow!

"It was like nothing I'd ever experienced," he said, "not with Felice, not with Joanie, never! I just looked at her, and something came over me, and I knew. I just knew. I knew not only that I had instantly fallen in love with her, but I also knew that this was the one, the woman I was meant to be with, the love of my life, the love that was gonna last forever. And it wasn't just me. She felt it, too. We had this immediate heat—it felt like sparks were going off when I touched her hand, like a thunderbolt when we kissed. It was the most powerful sense of connectedness I had ever experienced—and we'd just met! We ended up sleeping with each other that night, and we got married two months later. That was 15 years ago."

While the tale of Doug's love life was intriguing, and while I was certainly pleased for him that things turned out the way they did, I was having difficulty figuring out why he thought his story had any bearing on my situation.

"I'm really happy for you, Doug, but I'm not quite sure I've grasped the 'little secret' in all that."

"That's because I'm not finished," he said. "You see, in spite of all the magic and the fireworks at the start—all the chemistry, all the electricity that made us feel like we were destined to be together—by the end of our first year of marriage, guess what? We could scarcely put up with each other. Somewhere during those first twelve months, the fever just broke—the heat wore off—and in a relatively short period of time we went from craving each other to barely tolerating each other. And it's been a consistently negative slide ever since, to the point where I think it's no exaggeration to say that I actually hate the woman. And I have no doubt that she hates me, too. In our 15 years together, I've probably packed my bags to leave a dozen times, if not more."

I was stunned. Doug and Sandy seemed like such a nice couple, and while I certainly knew from my own experience that one should never make assumptions on the basis of outward appearances, still, nothing about the way they conducted themselves revealed even a hint of any discord between them.

I asked what I thought was the logical and obvious question—"Then why are you still together?"—but Doug reacted with a shake of his head and a scornful look that seemed to say, "You're just not getting this, are you?"

"I haven't left," he said, "because after coming at this whole 'relationship' thing from every different direction—from the 'raising a family' direction, from the 'taking your time' direction, from the 'love at first sight' direction—I've finally figured it all out. And what I've figured out, my friend, is this: It's all the fucking same. Do you hear me? It's all the fucking same. No matter how you slice it, no matter how it starts, sooner or later, love fades. It slips away. It dies. Always. And when it does, the choice you have is *not* between staying in a dead-love relationship or leaving to chase the notion of a love that'll last forever—that notion's just a mirage. The choice you have, instead, is whether to stay in a dead-love relationship, or leave to go live by yourself, all alone.

"When it comes to me and Sandy," he said, "we both choose to stay because, as awful as it is—and it's plenty awful at times, believe me—when you get right down to it, neither one of us wants to live alone. Staying together is the proverbial lesser of two evils.

"As for you," he continued, "you go do whatever you want. But if you're leaving because you believe in some version of a blissful, magical, everlasting love, you might as well be chasing after the Tooth Fairy.

"That's the little secret," he said. "Love is a lie."

* * *

I was, of course, surprised by Doug's little side trip into relationship hell. Surprised, but not persuaded—not then, at least. The demise of my marriage was too new. My pain had not yet ripened into fear, and my optimism about a future in which I'd find a new and lasting love had not yet been corroded by year after year of failure.

He's wrong, I thought to myself. It's bullshit. Love is not a lie. Doug is just a bitter, tired man, unwilling to keep up the search, and afraid to be alone.

I felt so sorry for him that night—sorry for his rotten luck, sorry for his misery, and sorry that he'd resigned himself to an outlook that was so hopeless and, from my point of view back then, so obviously false. Notwithstanding that I was at the terminus of a very long and failed relationship—one that had been moribund for years—I did, still, at that time, believe in love. In fact, the decision to end my marriage was a confirmation of that belief, an affirmative rejection of a relationship devoid of love, and even though the period surrounding my separation and divorce was emotionally wrenching, I nevertheless retained at my core not merely a hopefulness, but an abiding sense of certainty that a real, true, forever kind of love was waiting for me just up the road. Doug's caustic, wounded glumness that night did nothing to diminish my basic optimism. Instead, I felt only a sadness for him, a genuine sense of pity that he could be so wrong.

The past several years, however, have intervened, and have tempered my assessment. Experience has educated me, hindsight has alerted me, and perspective has enlightened me. All have combined to make me realize that on the topic of the promise of an undying love, Doug might not have been so wrong.

After my divorce became final—when I was no longer merely a separated married man living apart from his wife, but was instead, officially, an unmarried person—a curious new dynamic emerged in my more personal conversations with married friends, both men and women. The group table-talk didn't change. All the interactive babble—the frivolous jabbering about my dating exploits that enabled my friends to be both spectators and experts on the subject of my alleged love life—all of that continued. But when the setting moved from the group table to the quiet corner—when the conversations became one-on-one—separately, and alone, my married friends started telling me things. Private things. Painful things. Things too sensitive to discuss with other married friends because, no matter how confidential a discussion may be, married people tend to share such conversations with their spouses, and the spouse who learns a confidence second-hand will often be less than disciplined about the constraints on turning secrets into gossip. Apparently, as a friend without a spouse—without a pillow mate with whom to share pillow talk—I could be trusted with painful secrets. And so, one by one, those secrets were revealed to me. Secret lovers, secret betrayals, secret longings, secret wounds. Sometimes, a husband would confide in me one day, his wife the next, neither aware of the other's disclosures. And while the process was no doubt cathartic for those friends who chose to reveal their private agonies to me, it was, for me, an illumination—the shining of a bright light onto a very dark truth, which was this: Many of my married friends (friends whose apparent marital bliss had, through the years, filled me with envy but also with hope) were silently, secretly miserable, and the source of their misery was love—its absence, its death, its unfulfilled promise, and an aching, melancholy memory of what it once had been.

Love ends. For a few (a very few—an infinitesimal few), it ends at death. For most of us, though, it ends sooner, much sooner, well before death cuts a parting swath. On one of my early post-marital dates, the woman—a 40-year-old divorcee—revealed to me that as she was walking down the aisle on her wedding day, she knew, in her head and in her heart, that she was making a mistake. Yes, she had, at one point, been in love with the man she was marrying, but the love had peaked long before the wedding, and had been trending steadily downward even as she stood there in her veil and her white dress and said, "I do." After a second woman, a few dates later, told a similar tale, I grew curious, and began to ask the question ("So, did you know you were making a mistake as you were walking down the aisle?") any time a woman, on our first or second date, started talking about her divorce. And while my sampling, though large, was hardly scientific, the anecdotal evidence was unambiguous: For a significant percentage of the divorced women I've encountered in my middle-aged single life, love ended—or was clearly headed for the chapel's exit door—even before the wedding vows had been uttered. And if the same is true for a comparable proportion of divorced men (and why wouldn't it be?), one must move beyond the obvious observation ("No wonder those people ended up divorced!") and ask a more fundamental question, a question applicable not just to all those who had doubts at the altar, but likewise to all the Dougs and Sandys, all the married men and women for whom love is a thing of the past, all the wounded, aching people, attached and unattached, for whom the hope and the promise of an unending love is but a bitter, disappointing, oversold lie:

What the hell is this "love" thing anyway?

* * *

I think I know the answer.

Bear in mind, I'm not a sociologist, and I'm not an anthropologist. I'm no Ann Landers, and I'm certainly not Dr. Phil. I've never written a dissertation, and I've never participated in a clinical study. Professionally, educationally, and scientifically, I possess no legitimate credentials—zip, zilch, zero—on which to base any valid opinion on the question of romantic love. All I have is a bucketful of first-hand experience. But the bucket is very large.

When I married my wife in my early twenties, I was, for all intents and purposes, a tabula rasa. Barely out of law school, barely old enough to drink, I knew nothing first-hand about grown-up love, nothing first-hand about living with a mate, and even precious little about myself. Oh, sure, I shaved and had hairy legs and was physiologically capable of fathering children, but emotionally, intellectually and philosophically, I was years away from maturing into a fully formed adult. I was a fetus.

My married years were my infancy, the formative years during which I developed some basic instincts, some rudimentary skills, and some fundamental biases on the topic of long-term love, but only within the insulated cocoon of my limited surroundings. Not until my marriage ended were all those instincts, skills and biases exposed to any practical lessons from the world outside.

When I separated from my wife, I was 40. As I write this chapter, I'm just days shy of 50. The past ten years have been an education.

I began that education wounded but hopeful. Certainly, the failure of my marriage had taken its toll, but the prospect of a fresh start filled me with an optimism that vastly outweighed any divorce-induced doubts or fears. As I began this journey of the past ten years—this quest for a fulfilling, ever-deepening long-term love—I was clearly more hopeful than wounded, and my early experiences reflected that imbalance. So what if I wasn't succeeding right away—the stories were entertaining and the women were plentiful. With a little patience and persistence, success was inevitable.

In fact, though, I was more wounded than I thought—and, as it turns out, a bit too hopeful. I dismissed Doug's dire warning in the beginning—dismissed it, but didn't forget it. Doug's admonition, my friends' shared secrets, the wedding-altar stories offered by so many of my dates—these all traveled with me as I trekked my way through the glib adventures of these past ten years, all barely having any impact in the beginning, like a mere speck of a cloud on the horizon, but crowding the blue sky more and more, day by day, so that with each new prospect, each new romance, each new failure, a slowly-widening feeling of doubt competed with a gradually-shrinking sense of hope.

Doubt and hope. Hope and doubt. Year after year, one lesson followed another, but through all the back and forth, all the trial and error of my hands-on curriculum, I simply could not reconcile the hope with the doubt—could not put a stop to the growing tension between my desire, on the one hand, for a deep and fulfilling love, and my fear, on the other hand, that the love would inevitably end—until one day, in a bolt of enlightenment that channeled and distilled all the lessons of the past ten years, it hit me. And with a clarity borne of chaos and confusion, I finally figured it all out for myself.

* * *

The basics of love are not very difficult to decipher, nor are they all that unfamiliar. In fact, earlier in these pages, after explaining my break-up with Erin, I offered a definition. I suggested then that love was a rare and intoxicating mixture of desire and affection, compassion and need, empathy and openness. I still think that's true. It's all of those things, and it's nothing less than those things. Without the pull of desire and the tenderness of affection—without the generosity of compassion and the vulnerability of need—without the understanding of empathy and the intimacy of openness—love cannot, and does not, exist. Remove any of these ingredients from the mix, and love is gone. But if two people share all the components—if two people, at the same time, share desire, affection, compassion, need, empathy, and openness—love is the inevitable result. The combination is, indeed, intoxicating—it causes us to lower our defenses just as thoroughly (perhaps more so) as if we were drunk or stoned. And the combination is, indeed, rare—which is why we don't fall in love every day.

But there's another basic about love that I left out when I wrote that definition, a liberating basic that reconciles the hope with the doubt, but which I've only now, ten years into this quest, figured out. It is this: Love doesn't have to last forever.

* * *

Doug was *almost* right. It's not "love" that's the lie. Love—when it happens—is as true as the sun. It's the "forever" part that's the lie—the notion that love, when it's real, is, by definition, everlasting. We grow up conditioned to believe that love is forever, and that a love that ends is therefore a love that has failed. And since most of us fear the pain, the embarrassment, and the stigma of failure, we understandably fear the end of a love. The truth, though— and it's time we came to accept it—is that love rarely lasts forever, and that, more often than not, the end of a love is not a failure. More often than not, the end of a love is just the natural culmination of a cycle we cannot control.

Every love has a lifespan. This is neither theory nor conjecture—it's a fact. Just look around you and you'll see that it's true. Look at your friends, look at your relatives, look at your colleagues—look at yourself. Loves among all of you have come and gone, but they've been no less real because they've gone. And while sometimes the lifespan of a love is shortened due to lack of care, most of the time the care stops only because the love has already completed its cycle of life.

Most loves don't last forever. On rare occasions, the love outlasts the lovers, but on most occasions, the love passes first. That's not a failure. Whether a love lasts for weeks or for decades, it's end is just a part of its unique, particular cycle.

And that's okay.

Love is not a promise, and one cannot promise to love. Love is a state. It's a condition. It's involuntary. No promise can keep it alive, and when it's over, no mere promise can bring it back. Nurture it, yes, because, as with any living thing, nurturing can prolong love's lifespan, but recognize, too, that no amount of nurturing can make anything last forever, and therefore don't accept the notion that you've failed if and when a love ends.

* * *

Doug has no love in his life not because love is a lie, but because he's afraid of living alone. Love has hardly been a lie to Doug (he's been a party to it three times already), he's simply chosen the satisfaction of his need for company over the possibility of loving again. I can't fault him for that. He's like most people who stay unhappily in a relationship long after the love has passed—they stay because the relationship satisfies some other, greater needs, and I certainly don't mean to suggest that those needs are not valid or important. But where Doug and the others err is in concluding that since love doesn't last forever, it's no longer worth pursuing at all.

* * *

When I started this journey almost a decade ago, I believed in the myth that the only real love was the one that lasted forever, and so as romance after romance reached an end, I came to see myself as engaging in a ten-year process of failure.

But I was wrong. I was wrong about the love, and I was wrong about the failure. The love I shared with Nora—though brief and hampered by distance—was real. The love I shared with Erin—two solid years filled with depth and devotion—was real. The love I shared with others—some mentioned in these pages, some not, and no matter how fleeting—has all been real. Each ended—each love of the past ten years completed its natural cycle, with no two cycles exactly the same—but no ending served to erase the fact that a genuine love preceded it. None of my loves of the past ten years lasted forever, but each of those loves was real. And for that, they were each a success.

And so where does that leave me now? Unlike Doug, I'm not afraid to be alone. Through that liberating sense of self-hood—another happy gift of the past ten years—I've learned to appreciate the simple pleasures of living without a mate, and so if love never finds me again, I'll be okay.

But I'm not giving up on love, either. It doesn't have to last forever.

ACKNOWLEDGMENTS

Though recounted as a first-person narrative, my journey of the past decade was hardly a solo affair. Several key individuals accompanied me on the way—some from start to finish, some at various points along the path—and for the roles they played they each deserve my heartfelt gratitude.

Thank you, first, to my children, Jason and Laura. Thank you for putting up with me, for understanding me, for respecting me, and for making me so proud of each of you. Romantic love may be fragile, but parental love is eternal. You are, each of you, love personified.

Thank you to Lisa Goldstein Ruderman, my friend for 45 years. It's not just that you've been laughing at my shtick since first grade—it's the deeper, more fundamental bond of a male-female friendship that first developed before hormones had a chance to interfere. Your comments and insight during my writing of the book were always exact and correct. You are a very loyal audience, a great editor, and my forever friend.

Thank you, of course, to Steve Cassel. When I first started therapy with you, my head was so far up my ass my neck had hemorrhoids. By the time we finished, I was probably just as clueless as when we started, but at least I was breathing fresh air.

Thank you to Terri Cahn for your enthusiastic encouragement as the book progressed. You laughed at all the parts I thought were funny, cried at all the parts I thought were sad, and all without any prompting from me. I don't know whether this book is really any good, but you always made me feel it was great.

Thank you to my agent, Lisa DiMona, at Lark Productions. Despite an existing roster of bankable authors and a dizzying schedule, you had the guts/vision/confidence to accept as a client a never-published, middle-aged writer with no platform and no credentials. With a hand both gentle and strong, and with effort both steady and tireless, you kept me focused and grounded, and taught me much about the real business of writing.

Thank you to Marty Karlinsky, a good friend and a brilliant New York lawyer, for connecting me to Lisa DiMona.

And, finally, thank you to the women whose paths I've crossed during the past decade or so. For the part you've all played in inspiring this book, and for making me a wiser, if not a better, person, I love each and every one of you.

Except Debbie (you know who you are).

Offer your comments on *Finding It Again*, and check out Kenn Shapiro's blog, at www.FindingItAgain.com.

Published by
February Press, LLC